500

desserts

500

desserts

the only compendium of desserts you'll ever need

Wendy Sweetser

SELLERS
PUBLISHING

A Quintet Book

Published by Sellers Publishing, Inc.
161 John Roberts Road, South Portland, Maine 04106
Visit our Web site: www.sellerspublishing.com
E-mail: rsp@rsvp.com

ISBN: 978-1-4162-0652-1
Library of Congress Control Number: 2011935636
QTT.5DBE

This book was conceived, designed, and produced by
Quintet Publishing Limited
6 Blundell Street
London N7 9BH
United Kingdom

Food Stylist: Wendy Sweetser
Photographer: Ria Osborne
Art Director: Michael Charles
Editorial Assistant: Holly Willsher
Managing Editor: Donna Gregory
Publisher: Mark Searle

10 9 8 7 6 5 4 3 2 1

Printed in China by 1010 Printing International Ltd.

contents

introduction

For many of us — whatever our age — the most eagerly anticipated part of a meal is a wickedly indulgent dessert. Whether it's dark and chocolatey, light and frothy, or warm and comforting, nothing can quite beat that first spoonful of heavenly sweet delight when a bowl of luscious trifle, mousse, or pie is placed in front of us. The word "dessert" comes from the French verb *desservir* meaning to "clear the table," but all dessert lovers will agree that clearing the table is the last thing on their mind when a dessert is about to appear.

Every country has its own favorite way of rounding off a memorable meal. In France, pâtisserie shop windows glisten with jewel-like fruit tarts; in Britain, memories of Sunday lunch at grandma's have created a lifelong fondness for steamed sponges and fruit crumbles; while the indulgent dessert capital of the world — the United States — has introduced the rest of us to light-as-air cheesecakes, melt-in-the-mouth chocolate brownies, ice cream, and whoopie pies.

Although desserts as we now know them first became popular in the seventeenth century, serving something sweet had been the favorite way to end a meal long before that. The Romans preserved fruits as sweetmeats; Tudor kings and queens of England enjoyed sugared almonds, jellies, and marzipan; while the Frenchman Marie-Antoine Carême became the first celebrity chef when he created elaborately sculptured desserts for the world leaders of the day, including Napoleon and Britain's King George IV.

rocky road cookies, page 207

choux ring with stawberries & blueberries, page 121

With the arrival of the nineteenth century, more and more chefs came up with new ideas and dessert trolleys everywhere began to groan under the weight of increasingly ornate confections. Some desserts were considered so special they were named after favorite celebrities. Peach Melba was created in the early 1890s by Auguste Escoffier, the head chef at the Savoy Hotel in London, for the celebrated Australian soprano Dame Nellie Melba. Another was Pavlova, a cloud of crisp-coated meringue with a soft-as-marshmallow center, that both the Australians and New Zealanders claim the credit for having invented to honor Anna Pavlova, the Russian ballerina, when she visited their shores.

No single book could hope to include a recipe for every dessert that's ever been invented. In the following pages of *500 Desserts*, you'll find lots of your favorites, given a new or unexpected twist. We hope you'll be tempted to try some previously undiscovered treats and be inspired to create new recipes of your own.

plum frangipane tarts, page 95

equipment

Most desserts in this book can be made using basic kitchen equipment, although if you're a keen and adventurous cook you might want to invest in a few extra items.

The basics are: mixing bowls of different sizes; measuring spoons, measuring cup, and scales (which are invaluable if you're doing a lot of baking); rolling pin; grater; wooden spoons; hand whisk; wire-mesh sieve; cutting board; small and large chopping knives and serrated knife.

Also, large and small saucepans; baking sheets; wire cooling rack; spatula; and finally, waxed paper, aluminum foil, plastic wrap, and baking parchment.

The extras include:
electric mixer
An electric hand whisk or freestanding food mixer makes light work of all sorts of time-consuming tasks, such as making meringues, whipping cream, whisking custard mixtures, creaming cake batters, and beating choux pastry.

food processor & blender
Food processors are useful for grinding dry ingredients such as nuts, cookies, and spices to a powder and also for puréeing fruits. Blenders work in a similar way, grinding and puréeing ingredients, but they require at least some liquid to be added to the mixture for them to work efficiently.

baking pans & ovenproof dishes

If you're going to be serious about making desserts, you'll need a variety of baking pans in various shapes and sizes. Loaf pans, round, and square cake pans, as well as springform pans, muffin pans, and pie or tart pans are essential for a baker.

Additionally, a few ramekins or other small ovenproof cups or dishes for baking mousses, soufflés, and custards are useful for quite a few of the recipes in this book and have many other uses.

serving plates & dishes

A selection of attractive serving plates, bowls, dishes, and especially small glass dishes of varying sizes will show off your culinary creations to maximum advantage. These needn't be made from the best china or cut glass — pretty side plates, plain wine glasses, inexpensive glass bowls will all work well. Remember that any dish that needs to go into the oven or under the broiler must be heatproof to a high temperature.

white chocolate torte, page 37

cinnamon meringue slice layered with caribbean fruits, page 117

ingredients

Think of all the things you love to eat — ice cream, chocolate, cake, fresh fruit, cream — and you'll find them in desserts. It's what makes them so irresistible!

butter & oil

I prefer unsalted butter rather than salted — and definitely not margarine - for all my baking. Occasionally oils are used, and my preference is sunflower oil because it's mild-flavored. It's also ideal when a pan needs to be greased.

chocolate

Choose good-quality chocolate whether you're buying dark, milk, or white. Dark chocolate that contains a high percentage of cocoa solids (above 70%) is generally too intensely flavored for desserts — 50-60% being preferable. The flavor of dark chocolate desserts will mellow if the dessert is prepared the day before. Milk chocolate should contain at least 30% cocoa solids. For cocoa powder, use pure unsweetened cocoa to give an intense chocolate flavor.

eggs

Although large eggs are used in the majority of recipes in this book, size is not crucial in most instances and medium eggs can be substituted if that's all you have available.

One exception is choux pastry, where medium-size eggs are the right size to give the soft texture needed for choux paste while ensuring the mixture still holds its shape. If too much egg is added, the paste will spread when it bakes in the oven and you'll end up with flat, doughy profiteroles rather than crisp, round golf balls.

extracts

When buying extracts, such as vanilla, peppermint, and almond, buy good-quality ones, which will make a real difference in the taste of the finished dish. Use them sparingly, as they are very strong.

flour & sugar

Use the flour called for in a recipe. I like self-rising flour for cakes, and all-purpose flour for pastries (except when making choux pastry — profiteroles — where white bread flour gives a better result). Cornstarch is used for sauces.

For sugar, granulated, light and dark brown, and confectioners' are what you'll need.

fruits

For cooking, use fresh fruit when in season; otherwise, use fruit that has been canned in juice rather than syrup. Also, use freshly squeezed citrus juices to get the best flavor.

blueberry muffin trifles, page 142

chocolate brownie gateau, page 212

gelatin

Powdered unflavored gelatin needs to be sprinkled over a little cold liquid in a small bowl, left to soak for 5 minutes so the granules swell, and then dissolved by standing the bowl in a pan of hot, but not boiling, water. Once completely dissolved, the mix is stirred into the other recipe ingredients. It is essential that the gelatin has fully dissolved; if not, you'll find lumps in your dessert.

reduced-fat products

The full-fat milk, creams, cream cheese, and yogurt used in the recipes can be replaced with reduced-fat alternatives in most instances. However, if low-fat products are heated — for example, half-fat cream in a sauce — they should not be boiled hard or the sauce will curdle.

salt

Some cooks swear by adding a pinch of salt to every dish, while for health reasons others avoid it altogether. The recipes in this book don't have added salt but if you generally add salt to a recipe, do so; the choice is yours. Alternatively, the unsalted butter used in the recipes can be replaced with salted butter.

brown sugar

During storage, soft brown sugar particles can stick together in clumps and become hard. To make the sugar soft again, tip it into a bowl, cover with a damp cloth, and leave overnight, or grind the sugar in a food processor to eliminate any lumps.

techniques

Mastering a few simple basic techniques is the key to producing perfect desserts every time.

melting chocolate

If chocolate is melted at too high a temperature, it will develop a white bloom as it cools and resets so care needs to be taken when melting it. To do this, break or chop the bar into small pieces, place in a heatproof bowl and stand the bowl over a pan of gently simmering — not boiling — water, making sure the bottom of the bowl is not in contact with the water. Leave until the chocolate melts, stirring occasionally until smooth. Alternatively, chocolate can be melted in the microwave on defrost setting in 30 second bursts, again stirring until smooth.

working with light sponge & mousse mixes

Before baking a light whisked sponge batter or leaving a mousse to set, tap the container the mixture is in on the work surface to allow any large air bubbles to rise to the surface and burst.

individual raspberry soufflés, page 74

whisking egg whites

The secret to perfect meringues and other dishes containing whisked egg whites is to whisk the whites to soft peaks first before starting to add the sugar. To begin with, add the sugar 1 teaspoonful at a time until the whites start to thicken and become shiny. The remaining sugar can then be added in a steady stream. If sugar is added too quickly, the egg whites will be unable to incorporate it quickly enough, resulting in the whites not whipping up to sufficient bulk and the sugar leaking out as syrup when the meringues dry out in the oven.

To make meringues that are dry and crisp all the way through, place them in the oven on its lowest setting for several hours so the liquid in the egg whites evaporates and the meringues dry out and become crisp. A pavlova is different in that it is "baked" at a slightly higher temperature so the outer shell becomes dry and crisp but the center is still soft and marshmallowy.

folding in egg whites

When folding in egg whites, it's important to do it gently so all the air you've whisked into the whites isn't beaten out. However, as the mixture you're folding the whites into is likely to be quite heavy, soften it first by stirring in a tablespoonful of the whites. Once incorporated, fold in the remainder of the whites using a large metal spoon and a figure-eight motion.

toasting nuts

Nuts can be toasted under a conventional broiler, in a dry frying pan over a low heat, or spread out on a baking sheet in a low oven. Whichever method you choose, watch the nuts carefully and turn them over from time to time, as they quickly go from golden brown to black and burned.

coffee meringue kisses, page 122

basic recipes

chocolate sauce

For a smooth, luscious chocolate sauce to serve warm or cold, melt 3 tablespoons (1 1/2 ounces) unsalted butter, 1 scant cup heavy cream, and 8 ounces chopped dark chocolate over low heat until the butter and chocolate melt, stirring until smooth.

For a chocolate fudge sauce to serve warm, heat 4 tablespoons (2 ounces) unsalted butter, 7 tablespoons (2 ounces) light brown sugar, and 2 ounces chopped dark chocolate gently in a pan until the chocolate melts. Stir in 7 tablespoons heavy cream until smooth, then simmer for 2-3 minutes.

fruit sauce or coulis

For a simple fruit sauce or coulis, purée 11 ounces of your chosen fruit with 2 tablespoons confectioners' sugar and 1 tablespoon lemon juice until smooth. Raspberry and blackberry coulis can be strained if you want to remove the seeds.

fresh custard

To make thick custard, measure 2 cups (1 pint) milk into a measuring cup and pour all but about 1/4 cup of it into a saucepan. Mix 6 large egg yolks, 2 teaspoons cornstarch, and 4 tablespoons (2 ounces) sugar with the milk left in the measuring cup until smooth. Bring the milk in the saucepan to a boil, pour into the measuring cup, and whisk with the egg yolk mixture until combined. Pour everything back into

thai coconut balls with watermelon, star fruit & pomegranate seeds, page 238

the saucepan and stir continuously or whisk over low heat until thick and smooth. If making the custard ahead, dust the surface with a little sugar to prevent a skin forming as it cools.

For a thinner custard, increase the quantity of milk to 2 1/2 cups (1 1/4 pint). For a richer custard, replace half the milk with light cream.

The custard can be flavored with vanilla, almond, coffee, grated orange or lemon zest, or 1 teaspoon unflavored cocoa powder, mixed with the egg yolks.

brown bread & hazelnut ice cream, page 178

ultimate chocolate desserts

When it comes to indulgence, there's really nothing better than chocolate, whether it's a dark and sumptuous mousse, a sustaining bread and butter pudding, or a light, creamy roulade with a tangy raspberry filling.

chocolate velvet ganache gâteau

see variations page 47

This is equally good served as a dessert or as a special cake to celebrate a birthday or anniversary. Let the ganache cool at room temperature rather than in the fridge.

for the cake
1/2 cup (4 1/2 oz.) plain yogurt
1/2 cup (4 1/2 fl. oz.) sunflower oil
1 cup (8 oz.) dark brown sugar
3 large eggs
2 1/2 cups (10 oz.) self-rising flour
1 tsp. baking powder
3/4 cup (3 oz.) unsweetened cocoa powder
2 tbsp. milk

for the ganache & filling
3/4 cup (6 fl. oz.) whipping cream
9 oz. dark chocolate, chopped
2 tbsp. apricot jam
chocolate sprinkles and chocolate candies,
   to decorate

To make the cake, grease an 8-inch springform pan and line base and sides with baking parchment. Preheat oven to 325°F. Put yogurt, oil, sugar, and eggs in a mixing bowl. Whisk together until smooth and evenly combined. Sift in flour, baking powder, and cocoa, then fold in gently with a large metal spoon. Pour mixture into prepared pan and bake for about 40-45 minutes or until a toothpick inserted in the center comes out clean. Let cool in pan for 10 minutes, then turn out onto a wire rack to cool completely. To make the ganache, bring cream to a boil in a small pan. Remove from heat and stir in chocolate until it melts. Beat with a wooden spoon until mixture is smooth, then let cool at room temperature until thick enough to spread, stirring occasionally. Whisk for 1-2 minutes until light and creamy. Split cake in half through the center. Spread bottom layer with apricot jam. Place second layer on top and spread top and sides with chocolate ganache. Decorate with chocolate sprinkles and chocolate truffles. The cake will keep in the refrigerator for several days.

Serves 12

molten chocolate cakes

see variations page 48

A classic chocolate dessert that's rich, dark, and oh so satisfying. It's important to serve the cakes as soon as they come out of the oven so the soft gooey centers don't overcook and become dry.

canola oil, for greasing
6 oz. dark chocolate, chopped
1/2 cup whipping cream
3 large eggs

3 tbsp. dark brown sugar
1/2 tsp. vanilla extract
1 tbsp. flour
cocoa powder, to dust

Preheat oven to 425°F. Grease four 1/2-cup ramekins with a little canola oil and line the bases with a round of baking parchment. Put chocolate and cream in a large bowl and set the bowl over a pan of simmering water. Leave until chocolate has melted, then stir until smooth. In another bowl, whisk eggs, sugar, vanilla, and flour together until evenly mixed.

Gradually beat in the (still warm) melted chocolate. Spoon or pour mixture into prepared ramekins and set them on a baking sheet. Bake for 10 minutes or until set on the outside but still quite soft in the center. Turn the cakes out onto serving plates, and serve at once.

Serves 4

white & dark zebra creams

see variations page 49

An eye-catching variation on traditional chocolate mousse. Use good-quality dark chocolate but not one with a high percentage of cocoa solids or the flavor will be too bitter.

1/2 cup full-fat sour cream
1 cup heavy cream
2 oz. white chocolate, chopped
6 oz. dark chocolate, chopped

2 egg whites
2 tbsp. light brown sugar
grated dark and white chocolate and
    chocolate curls, to decorate

Heat sour cream and heavy cream together in a pan until they just come to a boil. Pour about one-third of the hot mixture into a bowl and stir in white chocolate until melted. Stir dark chocolate into the larger quantity of hot cream until melted. Leave both to cool.

Whisk egg whites until soft peak stage and then gradually whisk in sugar until stiff. Fold about one-third of the whites into the white chocolate mixture and the rest into the dark.

Spoon half the dark chocolate mixture into 4 glass dessert dishes or tumblers and chill for about 30 minutes until just set. Spoon the white chocolate mixture on top and return to the refrigerator for another 30 minutes or until just set. Spoon the remaining dark chocolate mixture on top and chill for 1 hour or until ready to serve. To serve, decorate with grated dark and white chocolate and chocolate curls.

Serves 4

bitter chocolate tart with toasted hazelnut crust

see variations page 50

This is a deliciously smooth, dark chocolate tart that can be served warm or cold.

for the pastry
2 tbsp. (1 oz.) finely ground toasted hazelnuts
1 3/4 cups (6 oz.) flour
6 tbsp. (3 oz.) unsalted butter, cut into
    small pieces
1 tbsp. confectioners' sugar
1 large egg yolk
about 1 tbsp. cold water

for the filling
7 oz. dark chocolate, chopped
9 tbsp. (4 1/2 oz.) unsalted butter
2 large eggs
2 large egg yolks
1/4 cup (2 oz.) dark brown sugar
7 tbsp. (2 oz.) cocoa powder
1/2 cup hot water
2 tbsp. (1 oz.) chopped toasted hazelnuts

In a food processor, blend hazelnuts, flour, and butter until mixture resembles bread crumbs. Add confectioners' sugar, egg yolk, and water. Blend until dough comes together in a ball. Wrap in plastic wrap and chill for 30 minutes. Preheat oven to 400°F. Roll out pastry on a floured surface and use it to line a 7x11-inch pan. Line pastry with waxed paper, fill with baking beans, and bake for 20 minutes, removing beans and paper after 15 minutes. Remove pan from oven and reduce temperature to 300°F. To make the filling, melt chocolate and butter in the microwave on low for about 5 minutes. Stir until smooth. In another bowl, beat eggs, egg yolks, and brown sugar. Fold into melted mixture. Whisk cocoa powder into hot water, then fold into chocolate mixture until combined. Pour filling into crust and bake for 10–15 minutes or until filling is just set. Serve topped with chopped toasted hazelnuts.

Serves 8-10

white chocolate torte

see variations page 51

Make this deliciously smooth and creamy cake in a pan with a removable base, as the finished dessert will be much easier to remove.

for the sponge base
3/4 cup (6 oz.) unsalted butter
scant 1 cup (6 oz.) sugar
3 large eggs, beaten
1 1/3 cups (5 1/2 oz.) self-rising flour
4 tbsp. (1 oz.) unsweetened cocoa powder
for the mousse
1 1/2 tbsp. unflavored gelatin
1 1/2 cups milk

7 tbsp. (2 1/2 oz.) cornstarch
1/2 cup (3 1/2 oz.) sugar
8 oz. white chocolate, chopped
2 tbsp. white rum
1 1/2 cups heavy cream
to decorate
extra whipped cream
chocolate malt candies

Grease an 8x12-inch cake pan and line with baking parchment. Preheat oven to 375°F. Beat butter and sugar until creamy. Gradually beat in eggs. Sift and fold in flour and cocoa. Spoon mixture into pan, smooth, and bake for 20 minutes. Turn out, peel off lining paper, and let cool on a wire rack. With a sharp serrated knife, cut horizontally through the sponge to make two layers. Wash pan, grease, and line again with baking parchment so paper comes slightly above sides. Place one sponge layer in pan. To make the mousse, soak gelatin in rum for 5 minutes, then stand bowl in a pan of hot water while you continue with the mousse. Whisk 1/2 cup of the milk with cornstarch. Heat remaining milk with the sugar until dissolved, and stir this onto cornstarch mixture. Return to pan, and stir over medium heat until thickened and smooth. Remove pan from heat and stir in chocolate until melted. Fold in gelatin and stir until smooth. Whip cream until it just holds its shape, fold into mousse, and pour over sponge base. Place second layer on top, chill until set, then decorate with whipped cream and candies to serve.

Serves 10-12

chocolate bread & butter pudding

see variations page 52

This dessert is a good way to use up bread that has started to go stale. White or whole wheat bread work equally well. Serve plain or dusted with confectioners' sugar, with custard (pages 24–25) or cream.

10 slices bread
5 1/2 oz. dark chocolate, chopped
6 tbsp. (3 oz.) unsalted butter,
    cut up
1 cup whipping cream

scant 1 cup (7 fl. oz.) reduced-fat
    crème fraîche
4 tbsp. orange juice
1/2 cup (4 oz.) light brown sugar
3 large eggs

Cut crusts off bread and cut each slice into 4 triangles. Put chocolate, butter, cream, crème fraîche, orange juice, and sugar in a bowl. Microwave on low power for 7–8 minutes, or place the bowl over a pan of simmering water until chocolate and butter melt. Stir until smooth. Beat eggs together in a large measuring cup, add melted mixture, and whisk until combined. Pour a half-inch layer into an 8-inch square or 9x12-inch ovenproof dish measuring about 2 1/2 inches deep. Arrange half the bread on top, overlapping the triangles. Pour half the remaining chocolate mixture over bread and arrange remaining triangles on top. Cover with remaining mixture, pressing bread down lightly. Cover dish with plastic wrap and leave in a cool place or the refrigerator for 4–5 hours. Preheat oven to 350°F and remove plastic wrap. Bake pudding for 30–35 minutes or until the top layer of bread is crisp and the chocolate mixture is set. Serve warm.

Serves 6

rich chocolate pots with coffee cream

see variations page 53

Chocolate and coffee are natural partners and combine together beautifully in this classic French dessert. Once the egg yolks have been added, transfer the mixture to a measuring cup to make it easier to pour into the ramekins.

for the chocolate pots
1 cup light cream
6 oz. dark chocolate, chopped
1 tbsp. dark brown sugar
4 large egg yolks

for the coffee cream
1 tsp. coffee extract (or 1 tsp. instant coffee
    dissolved in 1 tbsp. hot water)
1/2 cup heavy or whipping cream
chocolate-covered coffee beans, to decorate

Preheat oven to 300°F. To make the chocolate pots, heat cream and chocolate gently together in a pan until chocolate melts. Stir until smooth, then remove pan from heat and whisk in sugar and egg yolks, one at a time. Strain mixture into 4 ramekins or similar small dishes. Place them in a roasting pan. Pour enough hot, but not boiling, water into the pan to come two-thirds up the sides of the dishes. Cover pan with foil. Bake for 30 minutes or until just set. Remove, allow to cool, then chill for 1 hour or longer before serving.

To make the coffee cream, whisk coffee extract and cream together until it just holds its shape. Spoon or pipe the cream on top of the chocolate pots and decorate with chocolate coffee beans.

Serves 4

chocolate waves with dark chocolate mousse

see variations page 54

A chocolate mille-feuille that, instead of layers of puff pastry, uses fine waves of marbled chocolate to sandwich the rich and creamy mousse.

for the waves
6 oz. dark chocolate, chopped
2 oz. white chocolate, chopped

for the mousse
5 1/2 oz. dark chocolate, chopped
3 large eggs, separated
1/2 cup heavy cream

To make the waves, melt dark chocolate in a bowl over a pan of steaming water. Melt white chocolate in a separate bowl in the same way. Let both cool. Cut 12 pieces of baking parchment about 4 inches square. Lay chopsticks, wooden spoon handles, or pencils on a board, taping in place if necessary. Spread the dark chocolate over the parchment to about 1/2 inch from the edges, and while still wet, spoon the white chocolate into a small paper piping bag and pipe fine lines back and forth across the dark chocolate. Pull the tip of a toothpick through the white chocolate lines to make a feathered pattern. Lay parchment pieces over chopsticks so the chocolate sets in waves. When set, carefully peel away the parchment. To make the mousse, melt chocolate until smooth and beat in egg yolks, one at a time. In another bowl, whip cream until it just holds its shape, then fold it into the melted chocolate. Whisk egg whites until they reach soft peaks and fold into chocolate mixture. Transfer mousse to a bowl and chill for several hours. Place a chocolate wave on each serving plate and top with scoops of chocolate mousse and the remaining chocolate waves.

Serves 4

steamed chocolate sponge with vanilla custard

see variations page 55

For a warming winter pudding, nothing will beat these feel-good sponges.

for the sponges
1/2 cup (4 oz.) unsalted butter, cut up
4 1/2 oz. dark chocolate, chopped
3 large eggs
1/2 cup (4 oz.) light brown sugar
scant 1 cup (3 oz.) flour
4 tbsp. (1 oz.) unsweetened cocoa powder,
    plus extra to dust

for the custard
1 cup milk
1/2 cup heavy cream
1 vanilla pod
1 tbsp. cornstarch
2–3 tbsp. sugar (according to personal taste)
1 large whole egg and 1 large egg yolk, beaten

To make the sponges, melt the butter and chocolate together in a bowl set over a pan of simmering water. Stir until smooth, remove, and let cool. Grease four 7-ounce ramekins or cups with a little oil and line the bases with parchment. Using an electric whisk, beat eggs and sugar until thick and creamy, about 10 minutes. Sift in flour and cocoa powder and fold to combine. Pour in chocolate mixture and gently fold. Spoon mixture into prepared dishes and cover with foil. Steam in a covered basket or colander over boiling water for 45 minutes or until sponges feel firm. To make the custard, blend 4 tablespoons of the milk with the cornstarch. Pour remaining milk and cream into a pan. Split vanilla pod lengthwise and scrape seeds into the pan. Bring almost to a boil, then pour onto cornstarch mixture, stirring all the time. Return mixture to pan over medium heat and stir until thickened. Whisk in sugar and beaten egg and strain into a serving pitcher. Turn out sponges on serving plates and peel off paper. Serve hot, dusted with cocoa powder, topped with custard.
Serves 4

chocolate almond tuile baskets with chocolate-dipped strawberries

see variations page 56

The tuile recipe will make more than you need, so store the extras to serve with coffee.

for the tuile baskets
6 tbsp. (3 oz.) unsalted butter
1/2 cup (4 oz.) sugar
2 egg whites, lightly beaten
scant 1 cup (3 oz.) flour
1 tsp. unsweetened cocoa powder
2 tbsp. toasted flaked almonds

for the strawberries & cream
3 oz. white chocolate
16 large or 24 small whole strawberries
4 oz. milk chocolate, chopped
1 cup heavy cream
chocolate shavings, to decorate

Line two baking sheets with baking parchment and draw two 5-inch circles on each. Preheat oven to 400°F. To make the tuile baskets, beat butter and sugar together until creamy. Beat in the egg whites, adding one third at a time with a little of the flour. Fold in rest of flour with the cocoa. Finally stir in the almonds. Spoon 2 teaspoons of the mixture onto each marked circle and spread it out in a thin layer with a palette knife. Bake one pan at a time for 5–6 minutes. Immediately lift tuiles off pan, peel off parchment, and shape each into a basket using a small bowl as a mold. Continue with remaining mixture to make about 16 tuiles. To make the filling, melt white chocolate and dip strawberries in until half-coated. Put on a plate lined with foil and leave to set — not in the fridge. In another bowl, melt milk chocolate with the cream, stirring until smooth. Leave in a cool place until the chocolate cream can hold its shape. Spoon mixture into baskets, top with strawberries, and decorate with chocolate shavings.

Serves 8

chocolate roulade with chocolate cream & raspberries

see variations page 57

Roulades make impressive and popular desserts and are ideal for parties because they can be made ahead and need no last-minute attention.

for the roulade
6 large eggs, separated
3/4 cup (5 1/2 oz.) granulated sugar
7 tbsp. (2 oz.) unsweetened cocoa powder,
    sifted

for the chocolate cream & decoration
3/4 cup (6 fl. oz.) full-fat crème fraîche
9 oz. white chocolate, chopped
1 tsp. vanilla extract
6 oz. fresh raspberries
chocolate shapes and grated white chocolate,
    to decorate

To make the roulade, preheat the oven to 350°F. Grease a 9x13-inch jellyroll pan and line with baking parchment. In a large bowl, whisk egg yolks and sugar until thick and pale. In another bowl, whisk egg whites to soft peaks. Fold whites into egg yolk mixture with the cocoa. Pour mixture into the prepared pan and level. Bake for 20 minutes or until springy to the touch. Cool for 5 minutes in pan. Turn out onto a sheet of baking parchment and peel off lining paper. Roll up with the parchment inside and place on a wire rack to cool. To make chocolate cream, in a pan bring crème fraîche to a boil. Remove from heat, stir in chopped chocolate, and leave until melted. Add vanilla and beat with a wooden spoon until smooth. Let cool until thickened, and then whisk until light and creamy. Unroll roulade, discard paper, and spread with one-third of the chocolate cream to about 1 inch of the edges. Scatter most of the raspberries over the cream, saving a few. Roll up roulade and spread with remaining chocolate cream. Decorate with raspberries, chocolate shapes, and white chocolate.
Serves 8

variations

chocolate velvet ganache gâteau

see base recipe page 29

red velvet gâteau
Prepare basic recipe, adding 2 tablespoons red paste food coloring to yogurt and eggs, making the ganache with white chocolate, and replacing apricot jam with strawberry jam. Decorate top with fresh strawberries.

apricot & chocolate velvet gâteau
Prepare basic recipe, adding chopped fresh apricots between layers.

chocolate box gâteau
Prepare basic recipe, replacing ganache with chocolate buttercream made by beating together 1 cup (8 oounces) unsalted butter, 1 1/2 cups (7 ounces) sifted confectioners' sugar, and 4 tablespoons (1 ounce) cocoa powder. Press chocolate ladyfingers around sides of gâteau and top with chocolates or other sweets.

chocolate & brandy truffle gâteau
For adults, prepare basic recipe, pricking cake layers with a skewer and spooning brandy or Amaretto Disaronno liqueur over them before sandwiching with apricot jam. Decorate with chocolate brandy truffles.

chocolate & blueberry cream gâteau
Prepare basic recipe, replacing apricot preserves with whipped cream and blueberry jam. Spread top with whipped cream and scatter blueberries on top.

variations

molten chocolate cakes

see base recipe page 30

molten chocolate & yogurt puddings
For a less rich flavor, prepare basic recipe, replacing whipping cream with crème fraîche or Greek yogurt. Serve with fruit compote.

molten mocha puddings
Prepare basic recipe, replacing vanilla extract with 1 teaspoon coffee flavoring and adding 2 tablespoons coffee liqueur to chocolate mixture.

molten chocolate & orange puddings
Prepare basic recipe, replacing vanilla extract with the finely grated zest of 1 orange. Scatter over 2 tablespoons finely chopped pistachios before serving.

molten chocolate & chile puddings
Prepare basic recipe, omitting vanilla extract and adding 1 seeded and very finely chopped red chile. More or less chile can be added according to personal taste, but, remember, the smaller the chile, the hotter it usually is!

molten chocolate & marshmallow puddings
Prepare basic recipe, spooning the mixture into slightly larger ramekins (about 2/3 cup). Press a marshmallow into the center of each one, making sure they are completely immersed in the chocolate mixture, before baking.

variations

white & dark zebra creams

see base recipe page 33

minty zebra creams
Prepare basic recipe, stirring 1 teaspoon finely chopped fresh mint into the dark chocolate.

zebra cream swirls
Prepare basic recipe, dividing hot creams equally between two bowls and stirring 3 ounces dark chocolate into one and 3 ounces white chocolate into the other. Add in alternate spoonfuls to the glasses and swirl with a skewer.

zebra creams with toasted pecans
Prepare basic recipe, sprinkling a thin layer of chopped toasted pecans between each layer and topping with more chopped nuts.

zigzag zebra creams
Prepare basic recipe. Place several food cans on their side in the refrigerator. Holding each glass at an angle, spoon in half the dark mixture and then prop against the cans. Leave until starting to set, remove from refrigerator, and holding glasses on opposite angle, spoon in white mixture. Set again, add remaining dark mixture on top and stand glasses upright.

orange zebra creams
Prepare basic recipe, stirring grated zest of 1 orange into dark chocolate.

variations

bitter chocolate tart with toasted hazelnut crust

see base recipe page 34

bitter chocolate & ginger tart with cinnamon crust
Prepare basic recipe, omitting hazelnuts in the pastry and adding 1/4 cup flour and 1 teaspoon ground cinnamon to the pastry. Stir 1 tablespoon finely chopped preserved stem ginger into melted chocolate and butter when making the filling.

bitter chocolate tart with chocolate crust
Prepare basic recipe, replacing 1 tablespoon flour in pastry with cocoa.

mocha tart with hazelnut crust
Prepare basic recipe, serving the tart cold, topped with whipped cream flavored with coffee extract, Tia Maria, Kahlúa, or brandy. Sprinkle toasted hazelnuts on top.

bitter chocolate tart with crumb crust
Prepare basic recipe, replacing pastry with a graham cracker or chocolate crumb crust. Chill while preparing filling, and omit baking blind.

bitter chocolate tarts with walnut crust
Prepare basic recipe, replacing toasted ground hazelnuts in pastry with walnuts, and hazelnuts on top with walnuts.

variations

white chocolate torte

see base recipe page 37

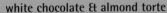

white chocolate & almond torte
Prepare basic recipe, replacing cocoa powder in sponge base with
ground almonds.

milk chocolate torte
Prepare basic recipe, replacing white chocolate in the mousse with good-quality
milk chocolate and replacing rum with Irish cream liqueur or orange juice.

white chocolate torte with a crumb crust
Prepare basic recipe, replacing sponge base with your favorite cookie crumb
crust. Press two-thirds of crumbs over bottom of pan, chill for 30 minutes, and
then pour mousse mixture on top when set, gently press rest of crumbs on top.

white chocolate & strawberry torte
Prepare basic recipe, replacing 1/2 cream in the filling with 8 large strawberries
puréed with 2 tablespoons orange juice. Whip remaining cream until just holding
its shape, then fold in strawberry purée.

dark chocolate torte
Prepare basic recipe, replacing white chocolate in mousse with dark chocolate
and the dark chocolate for decoration with white chocolate.

variations

chocolate bread & butter pudding

see base recipe page 38

chocolate brioche pudding
Prepare basic recipe, replacing the bread with slices of brioche or panettone.

chocolate bread & butter pudding with dried fruits
Prepare basic recipe, scattering 3/4 cup (4 ounces) chopped pitted prunes, dried cranberries, or a mixture of the two, over the first layer of bread triangles before pouring in remaining cream mixture and topping with remaining bread.

chocolate & pear bread & butter pudding
Prepare basic recipe, scattering 2 chopped pear halves (canned or fresh) over the first layer of bread triangles before pouring in remaining cream mixture and adding remaining bread.

nutty chocolate bread & butter pudding
Prepare basic recipe, sprinkling 1/2 cup (2 ounces) chopped walnuts or pecans on top before baking.

orange, banana & chocolate bread & butter pudding
Prepare basic recipe, arranging 1 sliced banana and segments of 1 orange over the first layer of bread triangles before pouring in remaining cream mixture and adding remaining bread.

variations

rich chocolate pots with coffee cream

see base recipe page 41

double chocolate pots with coffee cream
Prepare basic recipe for chocolate pots, heating half the light cream with
3 ounces dark chocolate and the other half with 3 ounces white chocolate. Add
alternating spoonfuls of chocolate mixtures to ramekins and swirl before baking.

rich chocolate pots with chocolate cream
Prepare basic recipe for the coffee cream, replacing coffee extract with
2 teaspoons unsweetened cocoa powder dissolved in 1 tablespoon hot water.

rich chocolate & cherry pots
Prepare basic recipe for chocolate pots, using larger ramekins and placing
4 or 5 pitted cherries, raspberries, or banana slices in the base of each before
adding chocolate mixture. Use coffee cream or plain cream on top, if you want.

rich chocolate & coconut pots
Prepare basic recipe for chocolate pots, replacing half the light cream with
coconut milk. For the coffee cream, replace coffee extract with a few drops of
coconut flavoring. Decorate each pot with a sprinkling of toasted flaked coconut.

rich milk chocolate pots
Prepare basic recipe for chocolate pots, replacing dark chocolate with good-
quality milk chocolate and omitting the brown sugar.

variations

chocolate waves with dark chocolate mousse

see base recipe page 42

mousse-filled brandy snaps
Prepare basic recipe, replacing chocolate waves with brandy snaps. Melt
3 ounces sweet butter with 3 ounces sugar and 1/4 cup light corn syrup.
Add 3 ounces flour, 1/2 teaspoon ground ginger, and 1 teaspoon lemon zest.
Drop 12 small spoonfuls of mixture on parchment-lined baking sheets and
bake at 350°F for 7–10 minutes. Cool for 1–2 minutes, shape as for waves.

white chocolate mousse waves
Prepare basic recipe, using white chocolate and 1 teaspoon vanilla extract.

chocolate mousse & strawberry stacks
Prepare basic recipe, spooning dark chocolate onto twelve 3 1/2-inch circles
drawn on parchment, feathering with white chocolate, and laying flat to set.
Sandwich in layers with mousse and sliced strawberries.

mousse-filled chocolate baskets
Prepare basic recipe, spooning dark chocolate onto four 6-inch circles drawn
on parchment. Feather with white chocolate, lift into shallow bowls and let
set. Peel off parchment and fill "baskets" with mousse and fresh fruits.

mousse-filled chocolate & almond waves
Prepare basic recipe, sprinkling dark chocolate with chopped almonds.

variations

steamed chocolate sponge with vanilla custard

see base recipe page 44

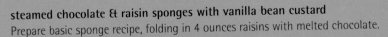

steamed chocolate & raisin sponges with vanilla bean custard
Prepare basic sponge recipe, folding in 4 ounces raisins with melted chocolate.

steamed chocolate sponges with chocolate custard
Prepare basic custard recipe, beating 1 ounce cocoa powder with egg.

steamed chocolate chip sponges with vanilla bean custard
Prepare basic sponge recipe, omitting dark chocolate and melting the butter on
its own. Fold in 4 1/2 ounces dark chocolate chips with flour and cocoa powder.

steamed chocolate & pecan sponges with vanilla bean custard
Prepare basic sponge recipe, folding 3 ounces chopped pecans into chocolate.

steamed chocolate & ginger sponges with ginger custard
Prepare basic sponge recipe, folding in 1 tablespoon finely chopped preserved
stem ginger with the melted chocolate. For the custard, omit vanilla and replace
sugar with 2–3 tablespoons syrup from the ginger jar.

variations

chocolate almond tuile baskets with chocolate-dipped strawberries

see base recipe page 45

nutty chocolate baskets with strawberries & cream
Prepare basic recipe for tuile baskets, replacing almonds with toasted chopped hazelnuts, pecans, or walnuts.

chocolate & glacé fruit baskets with strawberries & cream
Prepare basic recipe for tuile baskets, replacing half the almonds with finely chopped glacé fruits such as cherries, pineapple, or citrus peel.

chocolate tuile baskets with chocolate-dipped fruits
Prepare basic recipe, replacing strawberries with other fresh fruits (such as seedless grapes, kumquats, cherries on stalks, and/or pineapple pieces blotted dry with paper toweling), dipped halfway in white, dark, or milk chocolate.

chocolate tuile baskets with strawberries & dark chocolate cream
Prepare basic recipe, replacing white chocolate in the cream with dark or good-quality milk chocolate.

chocolate tuile baskets with strawberries & ice cream
Prepare basic recipe, replacing white chocolate cream with scoops of ice cream.

chocolate roulade with chocolate cream & raspberries

see base recipe page 46

chocolate roulade with strawberries & almonds
Prepare basic recipe, scattering roulade with 2 tablespoons flaked almonds before baking. Make half the white chocolate cream and use to fill roulade, substituting strawberries for raspberries. Omit cream covering. Dust with confectioners' sugar.

festive chocolate roulade
Prepare basic recipe, making the chocolate cream with dark chocolate and replacing raspberries with 4 ounces fresh cranberries simmered with a little sugar until they "pop." Decorate roulade with holly leaves and berries made of colored marzipan or gumpaste.

chocolate roulade with mixed berries
Prepare basic recipe, replacing raspberries with mixed berries and currants.

chocolate roulade with raspberries & milk chocolate cream
Prepare basic recipe, replacing white chocolate with good-quality milk chocolate.

chocolate roulade with apricots & cream
Prepare basic recipe, replacing white chocolate cream with 1 cup cream, whipped. Chop 5 apricots and fold into two-thirds of the cream, using this to fill the roulade. Cover with remaining whipped cream and decorate with apricot slices.

cheesecakes, sponges & hot soufflés

Creamy cheesecakes to linger over, sticky sponges
to keep out the winter chill, and hot puffy soufflés
that must be eaten straight from the oven: this
chapter has something for every occasion, whether
it's a formal dinner or a lunch with family
and friends.

citrus cheesecake with ginger crumb crust

see variations page 75

The easiest way to serve this creamy cheesecake is to cut it into slices with a sharp, serrated knife so the orange slices on top are separated into neat portions.

for the crust
7 oz. gingersnap cookies
6 tbsp. (3 oz.) unsalted butter, melted
1 tsp. ground cinnamon
for the cheesecake
finely grated zest and juice of 2 lemons
1 1/2 tbsp. unflavored gelatin
1 3/4 cups (12 oz.) ricotta cheese

8 oz. Greek yogurt
heaping 1/2 cup (4 oz.) sugar
2 large egg whites
for the topping
2 small oranges, peeled and thinly sliced
1 tsp. unflavored gelatin
1/2 cup freshly squeezed orange juice

To make the crust, grease an 8-inch springform pan and line sides with baking parchment. Crush cookies to make fine crumbs. Mix crumbs with melted butter and cinnamon. Press over base of pan and chill while you make the filling. In a measuring cup, combine lemon juice with enough orange juice or water to make 1/2 cup. Sprinkle gelatin on top. Let soften for 5 minutes, then dissolve gelatin by microwaving on low power for 3–4 minutes. In a bowl, beat ricotta cheese, yogurt, and half the sugar until smooth. Stir in lemon zest and dissolved gelatin. In another bowl, whisk egg whites until stiff, then whisk in remaining sugar. Fold whites into yogurt mixture and pour into crust. Smooth and chill for 3–4 hours or until set. To make the topping, arrange orange slices on top of cheesecake. Dissolve gelatin in orange juice (as you did before), allow to cool, then spoon juice over orange slices. Return cheesecake to fridge until set. To serve, transfer cheesecake to serving plate and slice.
Serves 8

sour cream cheesecake with honeyed apricots

see variations page 76

Ricotta makes this baked cheesecake beautifully light, but if you want something slightly heavier and creamier, replace half the ricotta with full-fat cream cheese.

for the crust
7 oz. graham crackers
6 tbsp. (3 oz.) unsalted butter, melted
for the cheesecake and topping
18 oz. ricotta cheese
scant 1 cup (6 oz.) sugar
4 large eggs

1 tsp. vanilla extract
8 oz. full-fat sour cream
for the honeyed apricots
6 oz. dried apricots, chopped
4 tbsp. honey
1 tbsp. lemon juice
1/2 cup (2 oz.) chopped walnuts

Grease an 8-inch springform pan and line sides with baking parchment. To make the crust, crush graham crackers until fine crumbs. Mix crumbs with melted butter, then press mixture over the base. Chill for 15 minutes. Preheat oven to 300°F. To make the cheesecake, mix ricotta with half the sugar, then beat in eggs one at a time, followed by vanilla. Pour this mixture over the crust and set pan on a baking sheet. Bake for 1 hour. Remove cheesecake from oven and let stand for 5 minutes. Stir remaining sugar into sour cream and pour over cheesecake. Return to oven for 5 minutes, then remove and let cool in pan. Chill until ready to serve. To make honeyed apricots, put apricots in a pan with honey, lemon juice, and walnuts. Heat gently until honey melts. Cut cheesecake into slices and serve with the apricots spooned over. Apricots can be served warm or cold.

Serves 6–8

layered lime sponge with lemon frosting

see variations page 77

Tangy, citrussy, and with a deliciously moist texture, this sponge cake makes a lovely summer dessert when served with a selection of fresh fruits.

for the sponge
11 tbsp. (5 1/2 oz.) unsalted butter
3/4 cup (5 1/2 oz.) light brown sugar
finely grated zest of 2 limes, plus a little extra
    to decorate
4 large eggs, separated
3/4 cup plus 1 tbsp. (3 oz.) all-purpose flour

1 tsp. baking powder
1 cup (4 oz.) ground almonds
for the frosting
12 oz. full-fat cream cheese
3 tbsp. lemon juice
1 cup (5 1/2 oz.) confectioners' sugar
fresh fruit, to serve

Grease and base line two 8-inch-round cake pans, which are 1 1/2 inches deep. Preheat oven to 350°F. To make the sponge cake, beat butter, sugar, and lime zest together until light and creamy. Beat in egg yolks, one at a time. In a separate bowl, whisk egg whites until stiff. Sift flour and baking powder into the creamed mixture and stir in along with ground almonds. Stir in a tablespoonful of egg whites, then fold in the rest using a large metal spoon. Divide mixture between cake pans and smooth tops level. Bake for about 30 minutes or until a toothpick pushed into center of each cake comes out clean. Cool in pans for 10 minutes before turning out on to a wire rack to cool completely. To make the frosting, beat cream cheese until smooth and softened. Add lemon juice, sift in confectioners' sugar, and beat until creamy. Spread one cake layer with some frosting, set other layer on top, and spread remaining frosting over the top. Decorate with lime zest and serve with fresh fruit.
Serves 8

baked strawberry curd cake

see variations page 78

Curd cake is a classic in England, where it is made with curd cheese (similar to American cottage cheese). To keep the fruit from sinking, let the mixture stand for 10-15 minutes before baking, giving it a chance to thicken.

for the base
7 tbsp. (2 oz.) pecans
6 oz. graham crackers
6 tbsp. (3 oz.) unsalted butter, melted
for the curd cake mixture
11 tbsp. (5 1/2 oz.) unsalted butter, softened
1 cup (7 oz.) light brown sugar
18 oz. ricotta or quark cheese
4 large egg yolks

1 1/3 cups (4 oz.) ground almonds
4 1/2 tbsp. (2 oz.) semolina
finely grated zest and juice of 1 large lemon
7 oz. fresh strawberries, hulled and coarsely
    chopped
1 tbsp. all-purpose flour
3 large egg whites
extra strawberries and confectioners' sugar,
    to serve

To make the crust, preheat oven to 375°F. Spread pecans on a baking sheet and bake for 7-8 minutes until lightly toasted. Let cool and chop into small pieces. Grease a 9-inch springform pan and line sides with parchment. Crush graham crackers, transfer to a bowl, add pecans and melted butter, and mix. Press mixture over base of pan and bake for 10 minutes. To make curd mixture, in a large bowl, beat butter until creamy, add sugar and cheese, and beat until smooth. Stir in egg yolks, one at a time, and add almonds, semolina, lemon zest, and juice. Toss chopped strawberries in flour and fold in. Let mixture stand for 10-15 minutes. In a separate bowl, whisk egg whites until they stand in stiff peaks. Stir 1 tablespoon into cake mixture before folding in the rest. Pour into prepared pan and bake for about 1 hour or until firm. Let cool completely before removing from pan. Chill until ready to serve. Just before serving, top with chopped or sliced strawberries and dust with confectioners' sugar.
Serves 10

banoffee cheesecake

see variations page 79

Leaving the cheesecake to cool slowly in the oven will help prevent the top from cracking, but if it does, just cover the cracks with cream when you decorate it.

for the crust
6 oz. graham crackers
1 oz. walnuts, finely chopped
4 tbsp. (2 oz.) unsalted butter, melted
for the cheesecake topping
3 ripe bananas, about 1/2 lb. unpeeled weight
juice of 1/2 lemon
5 tbsp. dulce de leche
3 large eggs

18 oz. ricotta cheese
7 tbsp. (3 oz.) light brown sugar
to decorate
1/2 cup (4 oz.) granulated sugar
2 tbsp. water
scant 1 cup whipping cream
1 tsp. coffee extract
1 small banana, sliced
juice of 1/2 lemon

To make the crust, mix graham cracker crumbs with walnuts and melted butter. Press mixture over base of a lightly greased 8-inch springform pan, and chill while you make the topping. Preheat the oven to 300°F. Peel bananas and roughly chop. Place in a food processor or blender with lemon juice, dulce de leche, eggs, ricotta, and sugar. Blend until smooth. Pour mixture into crust and bake for 50–60 minutes or until firm. Turn off oven and leave cheesecake inside to cool. For caramel decorations, line a baking sheet with parchment. Melt sugar with water in a pan over a gentle heat until dissolved. Bring to a boil and allow to syrup turn golden amber. Drizzle small shapes of caramel onto baking parchment with a spoon and let harden. When cheesecake is completely cooled, transfer to serving plate. Whip cream with coffee extract, then spread a thin layer over the top of cheesecake. Pipe or spoon the rest of the cream in swirls around the top edge and chill until ready to serve. Just before serving, decorate with caramel shapes and banana slices tossed in lemon juice.
Serves 6-8

sticky toffee sponges with fudge sauce

see variations page 80

A classic English dessert that's warm and comforting when the weather is cold. The soft crumbly sponge makes the perfect foil for the creamy fudge sauce.

for the fudge sauce
6 tbsp. (3 oz.) unsalted butter
1/4 cup (4 oz.) dark brown sugar
7 fl. oz. crème fraîche
6 tbsp. water
for the sponges
1/2 tsp. baking soda
2/3 cup (4 oz.) raisins

1 tbsp. molasses
1/2 cup boiling water
5 tbsp. (2 1/2 oz.) unsalted butter, softened
1/3 cup (2 1/2 oz.) dark brown sugar
1 large egg, beaten
1 cup (4 1/2 oz.) self-rising flour
1 tsp. ground ginger
1/2 cup (3 oz.) chopped walnuts

Lightly grease six 3/4-cup individual ramekins or cups. To make the sauce, put butter, sugar, and crème fraîche in a pan and add water. Heat gently until butter and sugar melt, then bring to a boil and simmer for 2 minutes. Remove sauce from heat and pour 1 tablespoon into each dish, reserving the rest. Preheat oven to 350°F. Put baking soda, raisins, and molasses in a bowl. Pour in boiling water. Stir to mix. In another bowl, beat butter and sugar together until creamy, then beat in egg. Stir in raisin mixture, flour, ginger, and 1/2 cup walnuts. Spoon mixture into dishes, place on a baking sheet, and bake for 35 minutes. Let stand for 5 minutes while you reheat sauce; they'll be easier to turn out after standing. Turn puddings out onto serving plates and scatter remaining walnuts on top. Pour reheated sauce over them and serve at once.

Serves 6

lemon & polenta sponge with blueberry sauce

see variations page 81

The secret ingredient in this light, fruity sponge is the whole lemons, which are gently simmered until soft, then puréed whole and folded in. It's best to use lemons with thin skins, as too much pith between the zest and fruit will make the cake taste bitter.

for the sponge
2 small lemons
3 large eggs
1 cup (7 oz.) light brown sugar
scant 1 cup (4 oz.) fine polenta
3/4 cup (5 oz.) semolina

1 tsp. baking powder
confectioners' sugar, to dust
for the blueberry sauce
1 pint (11 oz.) blueberries,
    plus extra to serve
2 tbsp. light brown sugar

To make the sponge, put lemons in a pan, cover with water, and bring to a boil. Cover pan and simmer for about 45 minutes or until lemons are soft. Drain and cool, then cut lemons in half and remove any seeds. Put lemons in a food processor and purée. Grease an 8-inch springform pan and line with parchment. Preheat oven to 350°F. Whisk eggs and sugar in a bowl until thick, creamy, and pale. Fold in polenta, semolina, baking powder, and lemon purée. Pour mixture into pan and bake for 45–50 minutes or until a toothpick inserted in the center comes out clean. Let cool for at least 30 minutes before removing from pan. To make blueberry sauce, gently heat about 3/4 of the berries in a pan with sugar, crushing with a fork or spoon until their juices run. Purée in a food processor, return to pan, and stir in reserved berries. Set aside until ready to serve. Serve the sponge, warm or cold, dusted with confectioners' sugar and cut into slices. Accompany with warmed sauce and blueberries.
Serves 8

butterscotch apple sponge

see variations page 82

Another English specialty that combines a fruit-topped sponge with a rich, toffee-like sauce. In England you'd make this in a "pudding basin." You'll need to use a heatproof bowl and cook the sponge in a steamer. Serve with extra stewed apples if you like.

for the butterscotch sauce
6 tbsp. (3 oz.) unsalted butter
7 tbsp. (3 oz.) light brown sugar
4 tbsp. (3 fl. oz.) corn syrup
1 tbsp. lemon juice
1/2 cup heavy cream

for the sponge
1 apple, such as Granny Smith, peeled, cored, and chopped
12 tbsp. (6 oz.) unsalted butter, softened
scant 1 cup (6 oz.) light brown sugar
3 large eggs
1 3/4 cups (6 oz.) all-purpose flour
1 tsp. baking powder
1 tsp. ground ginger

Grease a 1 1/2-quart heatproof bowl such as Pyrex. To make the sauce, heat butter, sugar, and corn syrup together in a pan, simmering gently until melted. Remove from heat and stir in lemon juice followed by cream. Spoon 2 tablespoons of sauce into greased bowl and set the rest aside. To make the sponge, add chopped apples to the bowl. In a mixing bowl, beat butter and sugar until creamy, then beat in eggs, one at a time, adding a tablespoon of flour with each one. Sift in remaining flour, baking powder, and ginger. Fold everything together until evenly combined. Spoon mixture into bowl and smooth the top level. Cover tightly with waxed paper and foil, and steam for 1 1/2 hours. Check water level in steamer regularly, and add boiling water as necessary. Turn out sponge on a serving plate, cut into slices, and serve with remaining warmed butterscotch sauce poured over.
Serves 6

pear & raspberry clafoutis

see variations page 83

Not strictly a sponge or a hot soufflé, this classic French batter pudding falls somewhere between. The fluffy batter mixture puffs up and becomes light in the oven and contrasts well with the sweet pears and sharper-flavored raspberries.

2 tbsp. (1 oz.) unsalted butter, melted,
    plus extra for greasing
3 ripe but firm pears, peeled, cored, and sliced
4 oz. fresh raspberries
scant 1 cup (3 oz.) flour

7 tbsp. (3 oz.) sugar
4 large eggs
1 1/2 cups milk
1 tsp. vanilla extract

Grease a 1-quart shallow ovenproof dish with melted butter and arrange pear slices and raspberries in it. Preheat oven to 375°F. Mix flour and sugar together in a bowl. In a separate bowl, beat eggs, milk, and vanilla. Gradually whisk egg mixture into flour and sugar until evenly mixed and you have a light, creamy batter. Fold in 2 tablespoons melted butter. Pour batter carefully into baking dish over fruit and bake for 40–45 minutes or until risen and golden brown. Serve warm on its own or with cream.

Serves 6

hot orange soufflé

see variations page 84

Not many desserts need to be served immediately after they come out of the oven, but soufflés most certainly do. If you delay, the soft, fluffy cloud will collapse.

2 tbsp. (1 oz.) unsalted butter, plus extra
   for greasing
2 tbsp. (1 oz.) all-purpose flour
1 1/2 cups milk
finely grated zest and juice of 1 large orange
heaping 1/2 cup (4 oz.) sugar
4 large egg yolks
5 large egg whites

confectioners' sugar, to dust
for the orange sauce
heaping 1/2 cup (4 oz.) sugar
1 tbsp. cornstarch
finely grated zest and juice of 1 medium orange
1 cup water
2 tbsp. (1 oz.) unsalted butter

Melt butter in a saucepan large enough for all the ingredients through the beaten egg whites to be incorporated. When butter has melted, stir in flour off the heat, then cook gently for 1 minute. Gradually stir in milk off the heat, then whisk continuously over medium heat until mixture is thickened. Stir in orange zest and juice. Stir in 3/4 of the sugar and scatter remaining sugar over the top. Grease 1 1/2-quart soufflé dish with melted butter. Preheat oven to 350°F. Beat egg yolks into cooled mixture one at a time. Whisk whites until stiff. Stir 1 tablespoon whites into mixture before folding in the rest. Pour mixture into dish. With a knife, cut through mixture about 1 inch from edge to help soufflé rise evenly. Bake for 45–50 minutes or until firm on top but springy in the center. While soufflé bakes, make orange sauce. Mix sugar, cornstarch, orange zest, and water until smooth. Heat gently, stirring constantly, until sauce is thick and smooth. Simmer for 30 seconds, then remove from heat and stir in butter and orange juice. When soufflé is cooked, dust top with confectioners' sugar and serve immediately with hot orange sauce.
Serves 4

individual raspberry soufflés

see variations page 85

If you don't have ramekins, you could use ovenproof tea or coffee cups or other containers with straight sides. The shape of the cups is important, because if the sides slope outward the soufflés won't rise properly.

10 oz. fresh raspberries
juice of 1 lemon
2/3 cup (4 1/2 oz.) sugar
1 1/2 tbsp. cornstarch, mixed with 2 tbsp. water
    until smooth

a little melted butter for greasing
3 large egg yolks
4 large egg whites
confectioners' sugar, to dust

Put raspberries in a pan, add lemon juice and half the sugar, and simmer for 2 minutes or until they are soft and falling apart. Remove from heat and push through a wire sieve to remove seeds. Return purée to saucepan and mix in cornstarch mixture. Cook over medium heat, stirring constantly, until purée is thick and smooth. Transfer to a bowl and set aside to cool completely. Preheat oven to 375°F. Grease six 7-ounce ramekins with melted butter. Stir egg yolks one at a time into raspberry purée. In another bowl, whisk egg whites until stiff, add remaining sugar, and whisk until glossy. Stir a tablespoonful of whites into raspberry mixture, before carefully folding in the rest. Spoon into ramekins, smooth tops level, and run a small knife around the top edge of each, between the ramekin and the mixture, to help soufflés rise evenly. Set ramekins on a baking sheet and bake for 8-10 minutes or until set and crusty on top but still soft in the middle. Remove from oven, dust tops with confectioners' sugar, and serve at once.

Serves 6

variations

citrus cheesecake with ginger crumb crust

see base recipe page 59

citrus cheesecake with oat & cinnamon crust
Prepare basic recipe, using oatmeal cookies and ground cinnamon for the base
rather than gingersnaps.

rich citrus cream cheesecake with ginger crumb crust
Prepare basic recipe, replacing ricotta cheese with cream cheese and half the
yogurt with heavy or whipping cream for a richer result. Whip cream until it just
holds its shape and fold in before adding whisked egg whites.

baked cheesecake with mixed citrus fruits
Prepare basic recipe, topping the cheesecake with a mix of citrus fruits such as
grapefruit, kumquat, and tangerine as well as, or instead of, orange slices.

citrus cheesecake with seeded crust
Prepare basic recipe, replacing gingersnaps with graham crackers for the base,
reducing quantity by 2 tablespoons and stirring in 2 tablespoons of seeds such as
sesame, pumpkin, poppy, or sunflower with the butter, omitting the cinnamon.

red fruit cheesecake with ginger crumb crust
Prepare basic recipe, topping cheesecake with raspberries or sliced strawberries
instead of orange and dissolving gelatin in cranberry juice instead of orange.

variations

sour cream cheesecake with honeyed apricots

see base recipe page 60

sour cream cheesecake with sponge base
Prepare basic recipe, replacing crumb base with sponge. Beat together
4 ounces sweet butter and 4 ounces sugar until creamy. Beat in 2 large eggs
and stir in 4 ounces self-rising flour. Bake for 15–20 minutes at 375°F.

sour cream cheesecake with honeyed mixed fruits & nuts
Prepare basic recipe for the honeyed apricots, using a mix of dried fruits
such as chopped pitted prunes, raisins, cranberries, or mango in place of
apricots; maple syrup instead of honey; and pecans instead of walnuts.

sour cream lemon cheesecake
Prepare basic recipe, replacing vanilla in the filling with the finely grated zest
of 1 lemon.

sour cream cheesecake with honeyed fresh fruits
Prepare basic recipe for the honeyed apricots, using fresh fruit such as
chopped apples, pears, or peaches instead of dried apricots, simmering with
the honey until softened.

sour cream cheesecake with peanut crust & honeyed apricots
Prepare basic recipe, replacing 1 ounce graham crackers with finely chopped
unsalted peanuts.

variations

layered lime sponge with lemon frosting

see base recipe page 62

layered lemon sponge with lemon frosting
Prepare basic recipe, replacing lime zest in sponge with zest of 1 large lemon.

layered lime & cashew sponge with lemon frosting
Prepare basic recipe, replacing ground almonds in sponge with ground cashews.

layered lime sponge with maple frosting
Prepare basic recipe, replacing cream cheese frosting with a maple-flavored one.
Heat 1 tablespoon maple syrup with 2 ounces sweet butter and 1 tablespoon
milk until butter melts. Sift 8 ounces confectioners' sugar and mix with melted
mixture until smooth. Cool, then beat with a wooden spoon or whisk until thick
enough to spread.

layered lime sponge with oranges & lemon frosting
Prepare basic recipe, adding segments of 2 oranges between cake layers.

layered lime sponge with citrus buttercream
Prepare the basic recipe, replacing the frosting with lime or lemon buttercream.
Beat 7 ounces sweet butter with finely grated zest of 2 limes or 1 large lemon
and 7 ounces sifted confectioners' sugar until smooth. Stir in lime or lemon juice
until soft and spreadable.

variations

baked strawberry curd cake

see base recipe page 64

baked raspberry curd cake
Prepare basic recipe, replacing strawberries with raspberries.

baked strawberry curd cake with lemon cream
Prepare basic recipe, adding a topping of whipped cream rather than dusting with confectioners' sugar. Whip 1 scant cup heavy or whipping cream until it just holds its shape. Lightly fold in 3 tablespoons lemon curd until it is just streaked with lemon curd. Spoon lemon cream over the cake, spreading in an even layer, and top with extra whole strawberries just before serving.

baked strawberry curd cake with a nutty crust
Prepare basic recipe, replacing pecans in crust with walnuts or hazelnuts.

baked strawberry & orange curd cake
Prepare basic recipe, replacing lemon zest and juice in curd mixture with zest and juice of 1 small orange.

baked peach curd cake
Prepare basic recipe, replacing chopped strawberries in curd mixture with chopped flesh of 2 peeled and pitted ripe peaches.

variations

banoffee cheesecake

see base recipe page 65

banoffee cheesecake with pecan crust
Prepare basic recipe, replacing walnuts in crust with finely chopped pecans (almonds also work well).

banoffee cheesecake with toffee sauce
Prepare basic recipe, and serve with toffee sauce. To make it, gently heat 3 ounces sweet butter with 6 ounces brown sugar and 1/2 cup corn syrup until melted. Simmer for 4–5 minutes, stir in 3/4 cup heavy cream and 1/2 teaspoon vanilla until smooth. Cool before serving with cheesecake.

banoffee cheesecake with dulce de leche cream
Prepare basic recipe, whisking 2 tablespoons dulce de leche into the cream for decoration instead of the coffee extract.

banoffee cheesecake with chocolate crumb crust
Prepare basic recipe, replacing graham crackers with chocolate chip cookies, ground to crumbs.

rich banoffee & orange cheesecake
Prepare basic recipe, replacing half the ricotta with cream cheese for a richer filling and the lemon juice in the filling with 2 tablespoons orange juice.

sticky toffee sponges with fudge sauce

see base recipe page 66

sticky toffee sponges with lemon cream sauce
Prepare basic recipe, replacing fudge sauce with a sharper-flavored lemon cream sauce. To make it, heat 1 1/2 cups light cream in a pan with the finely grated zest of 2 lemons and 2 ounces confectioners' sugar until sugar dissolves and mixture comes to a boil. Bubble gently for 5 minutes until the sauce thickens a little. Serve warm.

sticky toffee sponges with prunes
Prepare basic recipe, replacing raisins with chopped pitted prunes.

sticky toffee sponges with sweet spice
Prepare basic recipe, flavoring pudding with 1 teaspoon ground cardamom or ground cinnamon instead of ginger.

sticky toffee sponges with pecans
Prepare basic recipe, using chopped pecans instead of walnuts.

sticky toffee sponges with orange
Prepare basic recipe, replacing ground ginger with finely grated zest of 1 orange.

lemon & polenta sponge with blueberry sauce

see base recipe page 68

lemon & polenta sponge with crème fraîche
Prepare basic recipe, omitting blueberry sauce. Let sponge cool, then spread with crème fraîche and scatter top with toasted flaked almonds and blueberries.

orange & polenta sponge
Prepare basic recipe, replacing lemons with 1 medium orange or 3 clementines. Simmer orange for 1 hour (clementines for 45 minutes).

lemon & polenta sponge with strawberry sauce
Prepare basic recipe, replacing blueberries with strawberries.

lemon & semolina sponge
If you don't like the texture of polenta, omit polenta and use 9 ounces semolina.

lemon & polenta sponge with caramelized oranges
Prepare basic recipe, serving sponge with caramelized oranges instead of blueberry sauce. Remove peel and pith from 6 oranges. Slice fruit into thin rounds, removing any seeds. Gently heat 6 ounces sugar with 1/2 cup orange juice, orange liqueur, or water to dissolve sugar. Bring to a boil and cook to a golden caramel. Add orange slices and any juices they made and simmer for 2 minutes. Let cool.

variations

butterscotch apple sponge

see base recipe page 70

butterscotch pear sponge
Prepare basic recipe, replacing apple with 1 pear.

apple sponge with applesauce
Prepare basic recipe, replacing butterscotch sauce with applesauce. Over low heat, cook 1 pound peeled and sliced apples with 2 tablespoons water and 1 tablespoon lemon juice. When soft, mash and add sugar and butter to taste.

butterscotch apple & honey sponge
Prepare basic recipe. Replace 2 tablespoons sugar in the sponge with honey.

spicy butterscotch apple sponge
Prepare basic recipe, replacing ginger in sponge with ground cinnamon or pumpkin pie spice.

butterscotch apple sponge with maple cream sauce
Prepare basic recipe, replacing butterscotch sauce with creamy maple sauce. Melt 3 ounces sweet butter, add 5 ounces light brown sugar and 2 tablespoons maple syrup. When sugar dissolves, add 7 tablespoons heavy cream. Bring to a boil, remove from heat, and spoon 2 tablespoons into dish. Serve the rest warm with sponge.

variations

pear & raspberry clafoutis

see base recipe page 71

peach & blueberry clafoutis
Prepare basic recipe, replacing pears with 3 large ripe firm peaches or 3/4 pound halved pitted plums, and raspberries with blueberries or pitted cherries.

creamy pear & raspberry clafoutis
For a richer dessert, prepare basic recipe replacing 1/2 cup milk with light or whipping cream.

pear & raspberry clafoutis with sweet spices
Prepare basic recipe, replacing vanilla with 1 teaspoon ground cinnamon, pumpkin pie spice, or ginger.

pear & raspberry chocolate clafoutis
Prepare basic recipe, replacing 1 tablespoon flour with 1 tablespoon cocoa powder, dissolved in 1 tablespoon hot water, for a chocolate batter. Add the cocoa with the melted butter and fold in evenly.

pear & raspberry soufflé clafoutis
For a lighter, more soufflé-like batter, prepare basic recipe, separating the eggs. Beat just the yolks with milk and vanilla. Whisk whites until snowy peaks and fold in after the melted butter.

variations

hot orange soufflé

see base recipe page 72

hot orange & chocolate soufflé
Prepare basic recipe, drizzling 2 ounces melted dark chocolate over soufflé when it comes out of oven. Omit orange sauce.

hot lemon soufflé
Prepare basic recipe, replacing orange with 2 lemons.

hot orange soufflés in orange shells
Prepare basic recipe. Slice tops off 6 large oranges and scoop out flesh. Strain, use 4 tablespoons of the juice for the recipe, plus finely grated zest from the tops of the oranges. Cut a thin slice off base of each orange shell and stand them close together in a greased ovenproof dish. Spoon soufflé mixture into shells. Bake at 400°F for 20–25 minutes until risen and golden.

hot herby orange soufflé
Prepare basic recipe, stirring in 1 tablespoon finely chopped fresh basil or rosemary with orange zest and juice.

hot chocolate soufflé
For a hot chocolate soufflé, prepare basic recipe, increasing milk to 2 1/4 cups and omitting orange zest and juice. Stir 3 ounces grated dark chocolate into hot milk before adding sugar.

individual raspberry soufflés

see base recipe page 74

individual strawberry soufflés
Prepare basic recipe, using strawberries instead of raspberries. There is no need to strain the purée.

individual raspberry & mint soufflés
Prepare basic recipe, stirring 1 tablespoon finely chopped fresh mint into the strained raspberry purée before adding egg yolks.

individual raspberry soufflés with mango sauce
Prepare basic recipe, serving hot soufflés with mango sauce. Peel 1 ripe mango and put flesh in a blender. Add 1/2 cup freshly squeezed orange juice and blend until smooth. Add more orange juice to make a smooth sauce if the mango is large. Warm sauce and when soufflés come out of oven, place on serving plates, push a hole in the center of each with a spoon, and pour in sauce.

individual blackberry soufflés
Prepare basic recipe, replacing raspberries with blackberries.

individual fruits-of-the-forest soufflés
Prepare basic recipe, using a mixture of berries and currants of your choice. If not too many seedy fruits such as raspberries are included, there's no need to strain.

pies, crumbles & tarts

Well-loved family favorites that will never cease to impress. Whether your taste is for a simple fruit crumble, a wickedly rich chocolate and peanut butter pie, or light and crisp phyllo tarts, you'll find lots of irresistible ideas in this chapter.

strawberry cream pie

see variations page 103

A gorgeous taste of summer, this pie would be perfect for a party in the garden on a sunny day. Do not add the sliced strawberries for decoration until just before serving or juices will run from the fruit and spoil the appearance of the crème fraîche.

for the crust
11 oz. amaretti
3 oz. dark chocolate, chopped
1/2 cup (4 oz.) unsalted butter, melted
for the filling
8 oz. fresh strawberries, hulled and
   roughly chopped

4 large eggs
1/2 cup (4 oz.) sugar
1/2 cup heavy cream
for the topping
1/2 cup crème fraîche
extra strawberries, sliced

Preheat oven to 350°F. To make the crust, crush amaretti in a food processor to make coarse crumbs. Add chocolate and process again until mixture is quite fine. Transfer to a bowl and stir in melted butter. Press crumb mixture over base and sides of a 9-inch loose-bottomed flan pan or pie pan measuring about 1 1/2 inches deep. Place pan on a baking sheet and bake for 10 minutes. Remove from oven and push crust down with the back of a spoon if it has risen up. To make the filling, put strawberries, eggs, and sugar in a food processor or blender. Blend until smooth. In a bowl, whip cream until standing in soft peaks, then fold in strawberry purée until evenly mixed. Pour filling into crust and bake for 25 minutes or until set. Remove from oven and let cool completely before removing from pan. Spread crème fraîche over pie. Chill until ready to serve. Decorate with sliced strawberries just before serving.

Serves 8

deep-dish nectarine & blueberry pie

see variations page 104

A great dessert when you've got the family to feed, it's sustaining and deliciously fruity. The nectarines can be peeled before being added to the pie; just soak in boiling water for about 1 minute before allowing to cool and skinning with a sharp knife.

for the pastry
2 1/4 cups (8 oz.) flour
10 tbsp. (5 oz.) unsalted butter,
    cut in small pieces
2 tbsp. sugar, plus extra to dust
1 egg yolk
3 tbsp. cold water

beaten egg, to glaze
for the filling
about 6 ripe nectarines (depending on size),
    halved, pitted, and sliced
8 oz. fresh blueberries
1 tbsp. sugar

To make the pastry, sift flour into a mixing bowl. Rub in butter until mixture resembles bread crumbs. Stir in sugar. Beat egg yolk with water and add to bowl, mixing in to make a dough. Knead lightly until smooth, wrap in plastic wrap, and chill for 30 minutes. Arrange sliced nectarines and blueberries in a pie dish. Roll out pastry, cut a strip about 1 inch wide to fit around top edge of pie dish, dampen, and press in place. Lift remaining pastry over fruit, trimming edges with a sharp knife. Press pastry edges together to seal and mark a decorative border with the back of a knife. Gather up and reroll pastry trimmings and cut out leaves with a small sharp knife. Dampen and arrange these over pie. Cut a hole in pastry top to allow steam to escape. When ready to bake, preheat oven to 350°F. Brush pastry with beaten egg to glaze and dust with sugar. Set pie on baking sheet and bake for 35 minutes or until golden brown. Serve warm or cold with whipped cream or ice cream.
Serves 6

chocolate-glazed peanut butter & cinnamon pie

see variations page 105

Chocolate and peanut butter are a marriage made in heaven in this wickedly rich dessert. If you don't have a pie plate, use an 8-inch flan pan instead.

for the crust
7 oz. chocolate graham crackers
6 tbsp. (3 oz.) unsalted butter, melted
for the pie
9 oz. light cream cheese
3/4 cup (5 1/2 oz.) crunchy or smooth peanut
    butter

4 1/2 tbsp. (2 oz.) light brown sugar
1/2 tsp. ground cinnamon
1 cup heavy cream
2 tbsp. (1 oz.) unsalted butter
2 oz. dark chocolate, chopped
extra whipped cream, chocolate sticks or
    cigarillos and grated chocolate, to decorate

To make the crust, crush graham crackers to fine crumbs and mix with melted butter. Press mixture over base and up sides of a 9-inch pie plate. Chill while you prepare filling. To make the filling, whisk together cream cheese, peanut butter, brown sugar, and cinnamon. In another bowl, whip cream until it starts to thicken. Stir about two-thirds of the whipped cream into peanut butter mixture. Spoon into crumb crust and smooth out until level.

Put butter, chocolate, and remaining whipped cream in a saucepan, and heat gently until butter and chocolate melt. Stir until smooth, cool, then pour over the filling. Chill for at least 1 hour to firm. When ready to serve, decorate with extra whipped cream, chocolate sticks or cigarillos and a sprinkling of grated chocolate.

Serves 8

apricot–pistachio tarte tatin

see variations page 106

A variation on the famous French tart named after the sisters who, so the story goes, cooked their favorite apple tart upside down by mistake. When inverting the cooked tart onto a serving plate, be sure the plate is large enough to prevent any hot caramel splashing over your hands.

heaping 1/2 cup (4 oz.) sugar
4 tbsp. (2 oz.) unsalted butter, chopped small
18 oz. fresh apricots, halved and pitted

12 oz. puff pastry, defrosted if frozen
1/2 cup (2 oz.) pistachios
crème fraîche, to serve

Heat sugar and butter in a 9-inch ovenproof skillet or tarte tatin pan until melted, then cook to a rich golden brown caramel. Remove pan from heat and arrange apricot halves, rounded-side down, in pan almost to edge. Place first one at a slight angle and the rest butting up against each other and overlapping slightly to allow for shrinkage during baking. Work from outside into center, placing apricots in concentric circles until pan is full.

Preheat the oven to 375°F. Roll out pastry on a lightly floured surface to a circle the same size as the pan. Lift it over apricots, tucking pastry edges down the sides between apricots and pan. Prick pastry all over with a fork and set pan on a baking sheet. Bake for 25–30 minutes or until pastry is puffed and golden brown. Remove pan from oven and let stand for 2–3 minutes before inverting tart onto a warm serving plate. Tuck back into place any apricots that stick to the pan and scatter pistachios over top. Serve warm with crème fraîche.

Serves 6

plum frangipane tarts

see variations page 107

Frangipane is a sweet almond sponge mixture that is popular in France, where it is added to several classic desserts such as this fruit flan. If you don't have individual flan pans, make one large tart using an 8- or 9-inch pan about 1 inch deep.

for the pastry
1/4 cup (2 oz.) sugar
5 tbsp. (2 1/2 oz.) unsalted butter, cut up
1 large egg yolk
2 tbsp. cold water
1 3/4 cups (6 oz.) flour
for the filling
8 tbsp. plum jelly

1 3/4 cups (5 1/2 oz.) ground almonds
1/2 cup (3 1/2 oz.) sugar
finely grated zest of 1 lemon
3 large eggs, beaten
5 tbsp. sunflower oil
4 tbsp. freshly squeezed orange juice
8 plums, pitted and sliced
2 tbsp. chopped toasted hazelnuts

To make the pastry, put sugar, butter, and egg yolk in a food processor, and blend until smooth. Add water and blend again. Add flour and blend until ingredients are just combined. Knead dough lightly on a lightly floured work surface until smooth. Shape into a ball, wrap in plastic wrap, and chill for 1 hour. Bring back to room temperature before rolling out. Preheat oven to 350°F. Divide pastry into 4 pieces. Roll out each piece on a lightly floured surface, and line four 4-inch flan pans that are 3/4–1 inch deep. Place on a greased baking sheet. Spread 1 tablespoon plum jelly over the base of each pastry crust. To make the filling, whisk together ground almonds, sugar, lemon zest, eggs, oil, and orange juice until smooth. Spoon into crusts. Top with plum slices, pressing them down gently, and bake for 25–30 minutes or until almond mixture is golden and set. Remove tarts from oven. Warm remaining jam and brush over top of each tart. Sprinkle with toasted hazelnuts and serve warm.
Serves 4

cherry & custard phyllo tarts

see variations page 108

Once unwrapped, phyllo pastry dries out very quickly and becomes too hard and brittle to use, so work as quickly as you can, keep sheets you are not using covered with a damp cloth.

32 squares phyllo pastry, each about 4 inches
1/2 cup (4 oz.) unsalted butter, melted
for the custard
2 large eggs
1 large egg yolk
4 tbsp. (2 oz.) sugar
1 tbsp. cornstarch

7 fl. oz. crème fraîche
1/2 tsp. vanilla extract
for the cherries
12 oz. ripe cherries, pitted
4 tbsp. orange juice
1 tbsp. sugar, or to taste

Brush a phyllo square with melted butter and press gently into a cup in a muffin pan. Layer 3 more squares on top, brushing each one with butter, and angling the points of the squares in a star pattern. Repeat with remaining phyllo squares to make 8 tartlet crusts. Bake for 15–20 minutes or until pastry is golden brown and crisp. Remove from oven and cool for 10–15 minutes before lifting crusts from pan. Let cool completely. To make the custard, put eggs, egg yolk, and 3 tablespoons sugar in a bowl. Beat until pale, and creamy. Stir in cornstarch. Bring crème fraîche to a boil, then pour onto egg mixture, whisking constantly. Return mixture to pan and slowly bring to a simmer over low heat, stirring constantly. Cook gently for 2–3 minutes then remove from heat. Stir in vanilla and sprinkle remaining sugar over top of custard to prevent a skin forming as it cools. When cold, chill until needed. Put cherries in a small pan with orange juice and sugar, cover, and simmer gently for 10 minutes or until softened. Let cool. When ready to serve, stir custard well, fill phyllo crusts, and set on serving plates. Drain cherries and spoon them on top of custard.

Serves 8

french apple tart

see variations page 109

If you don't have a food processor, make the pastry by sifting the flour into a bowl and making a well in the center. Put the butter and egg yolk in the well and mix to a coarse paste. Draw the flour over egg mixture and chop through with a palette knife. Sprinkle with water and bring the dough together with your hands, kneading until smooth.

for the pastry
7 tbsp. (3 1/2 oz.) unsalted butter at room
    temperature, cut into small pieces
1 medium egg yolk
2 1/2 tbsp. cold water
2 cups (7 oz.) flour
for the filling
4 apples, such as Golden Delicious or Braeburn

3 tbsp. sugar
1 tsp. ground cinnamon
4 tbsp. (2 oz.) unsalted butter,
    cut into small pieces
for the glaze
4 tbsp. apricot jam
1 tbsp. lemon juice

To make the pastry, blend butter and egg yolk in food processor until smooth and creamy. Add water and blend again. Pour in flour and pulse briefly until dough just comes together in a ball. Transfer to a lightly floured work surface and knead gently until smooth. Wrap in plastic wrap and chill for 45 minutes. Allow pastry to return to room temperature before rolling out and lining a 9-inch loose-bottomed flan pan. To make the filling, peel, core, and thinly slice apples. Spread half the apples randomly over pastry, then top with remaining apple slices arranged in neat concentric circles, overlapping to fill shell completely. Sprinkle with sugar and cinnamon, and dot with butter. Preheat oven to 375°F. Bake tart on a baking sheet for about 50–60 minutes, or until apples are browned and pastry is golden. Remove from oven and let stand for 10 minutes before lifting tart from pan. Heat apricot jam and lemon juice together until bubbling. Strain, then brush mixture over apple slices to glaze.
Serves 6

kiwi, orange & white chocolate cream mille-feuille

see variations page 110

When you roll out the pastry, be careful not to stretch it or it will shrink back during baking and the mille-feuille layers will be uneven. Do not assemble these more than two hours before serving or the pastry will become soft.

12 oz. puff pastry
confectioners' sugar, to dust
for the filling
½ cup heavy cream

5 oz. white chocolate, chopped
2 kiwi fruit, peeled and sliced
4 oranges, peeled and segmented

Line a baking sheet with nonstick baking parchment. On a board dusted with confectioners' sugar, roll out pastry about 1/4 inch thick. Using a sharp knife, cut out 12 rectangles, each about 3 1/2x2 inches. Lift them onto baking sheet, dust with confectioners' sugar, and chill for 30 minutes. Preheat oven to 400°F.

Bake pastry rectangles for 5 minutes, remove from oven, and dust with more confectioners' sugar. Return to oven and bake for 5 minutes more or until pastry is risen and golden brown. Transfer to a wire rack and let cool. To make the filling, bring cream to a boil, remove from heat, and stir in chocolate until melted. Let cool, stirring occasionally. When thick enough to spread, whisk for 1 minute until light and creamy. Using a sharp knife, split each pastry rectangle in half horizontally, and spread or pipe chocolate cream over the bases. Top with fruit and pastry lids. Dust with more confectioners' sugar and chill until ready to serve.

Serves 6

blackberry & apple oatmeal crumble

see variations page 111

This crumble, with its crunchy oat topping and spicy fruit filling, makes a great family dessert.

1 1/2 lbs. cooking apples, peeled, cored, and chopped
finely grated zest and juice of 1 orange
1 tsp. pumpkin pie spice
2 tbsp. (1 oz.) sugar
8 oz. fresh blackberries

for the topping
1/2 cup (4 oz.) unsalted butter, cut up into small pieces
1 cup (4 oz.) flour
1 cup (4 oz.) chopped walnuts
1/2 cup (2 oz.) rolled oats
7 tbsp. (3 oz.) light brown sugar

Put chopped apples in a saucepan. Add orange zest and juice, pumpkin pie spice, and sugar, and simmer over low heat for 10 minutes or until apples have softened. Stir in blackberries taking care not to crush them. Spoon fruit into a 1 1/2-quart ovenproof dish and let cool completely.

To make the topping, rub butter into flour until consistency is like fine bread crumbs. Stir in walnuts, oats, and sugar. Spoon mixture over fruit to cover it evenly. Preheat oven to 350°F and bake for 35 minutes or until topping is golden. Serve hot with custard (pages 24–25).

Serves 8

variations

strawberry cream pie

see base recipe page 87

strawberry cream pie with graham cracker crust
Prepare basic recipe, replacing amaretti in crust with a graham cracker or chocolate graham cracker.

blueberry cream pie
Prepare basic recipe, using whole fresh blueberries instead of strawberries.

strawberry cream pie with strawberry sauce
Prepare basic recipe, serving with strawberry sauce rather than crème fraîche. Hull 12 ounces fresh strawberries. Purée 8 ounces in a food processor or blender with 4 tablespoons orange juice and 2 tablespoons confectioners' sugar. Stir in remaining strawberries, chopped in small pieces.

strawberry & lime cream pie
Prepare basic recipe, adding finely grated zest of 2 limes to filling. (You could use zest from 1 lemon instead, if you want.)

strawberry cream pie with chocolate cream
Prepare basic recipe, replacing crème fraîche topping with chocolate cream. Dissolve 1 tablespoon unsweetened cocoa in 1 tablespoon hot water, cool, then add to whipped cream.

variations

deep-dish nectarine & blueberry pie

see base recipe page 88

deep-dish pear & blackberry pie

Prepare basic recipe, replacing nectarines with pears and blueberries or raspberries if you prefer with blackberries.

deep-dish nectarine & blueberry pie with cinnamon whole-wheat crust

Prepare basic recipe, making the pastry with half whole wheat flour and half self-rising white flour and adding 1 teaspoon ground cinnamon.

deep-dish spiced nectarine & blueberry pie

Prepare basic recipe, adding 1 teaspoon ground ginger and 1/2 teaspoon ground cinnamon to fruit.

creamy deep-dish nectarine & blueberry pie

Prepare basic recipe, adding 4 tablespoons heavy cream to fruit.

deep-dish pineapple & blueberry pie

Prepare basic recipe, using 1 pound nectarines, 1 pound chopped pineapple (or mango), and the blueberries for filling.

variations

chocolate-glazed peanut butter & cinnamon pie

see base recipe page 90

peanut butter & cinnamon pie with chocolate sauce & ice cream
Prepare basic recipe, omitting chocolate topping (or using it if you really want the extra decadence). Serve with hot or cold chocolate sauce (page 24) and vanilla ice cream.

chocolate-glazed cashew butter & cinnamon pie
Prepare basic recipe, substituting another nut butter (crunchy or smooth) such as cashew for the peanut butter. Hazelnut, pecan, or macadamia butters would be equally good.

chocolate-glazed peanut butter pie with ginger crust
Prepare basic recipe, replacing chocolate crust with gingersnap crust.

milk chocolate-glazed peanut butter & cinnamon pie
Prepare basic recipe, topping the pie with a sweeter, less densely flavored topping by substituting good-quality milk chocolate for the dark.

chocolate-glazed peanut butter & cardamom pie
Prepare the basic recipe, replacing cinnamon in filling with 1/2 teaspoon ground cardamom.

variations

apricot & pistachio tarte tatin

see base recipe page 92

apricot tarte tatin with shortcrust pastry
Prepare basic recipe, using a sweet shortcrust pastry instead of puff pastry (page 84).

apple tarte tatin
Prepare basic recipe, replacing apricots with apples, peeled, cored, and thickly sliced. Pears would also work well.

apricot & almond tarte tatin
Prepare basic recipe, replacing pistachios with toasted flaked almonds (or chopped toasted pecans).

spicy apricot tarte tatin
Prepare basic recipe, adding 1 teaspoon ground cinnamon or ground ginger to the sugar and butter mixture.

mixed fruit tarte tatin
Prepare basic recipe, using a mix of different fruits rather than just apricots. Apples with blackberries tucked between, mango with sliced banana, and halved plums and pitted cherries all work well.

variations

plum frangipane tarts

see base recipe page 95

apricot frangipane tarts
Prepare basic recipe, substituting apricot jam for plum jam and apricots
for plums.

plum frangipane puff tarts
Prepare basic recipe, using 10 ounces thinly rolled puff pastry instead
of shortcrust.

plum & hazelnut frangipane tarts
Prepare basic recipe, replacing ground almonds in filling with ground
hazelnuts.

plum & cinnamon frangipane tarts
Prepare basic recipe, replacing grated lemon zest in filling with 1 teaspoon
ground cinnamon.

plum & sunflower seed frangipane tarts
Prepare basic recipe, scattering 2 tablespoons sunflower seeds over the
glazed tarts.

variations

cherry & custard phyllo tarts

see base recipe page 96

cherry & custard cream phyllo tarts
Prepare basic recipe, making custard with light cream or half cream and half milk instead of crème fraîche.

cherry & almond custard phyllo tarts
Prepare basic recipe, replacing vanilla extract in custard with almond flavoring.

cherry & custard puff tarts
Prepare basic recipe, replacing phyllo with about 9 ounces puff or shortcrust pastry. Roll out pastry thinly and line into individual, fairly deep, flan pans. Bake blind (using baking beans) until crisp and golden brown.

blueberry & custard phyllo tarts
Prepare basic recipe, replacing cherries in topping with blueberries or blackberries.

cherry & chocolate custard phyllo tarts
Prepare basic recipe, heating 2 ounces chopped or grated dark chocolate with crème fraîche until chocolate melts and crème fraîche comes to a boil.

variations

french apple tart

see base recipe page 99

french apple tart with puff crust
Prepare basic recipe, replacing pastry with 12 ounces thinly rolled
puff pastry.

spice-glazed french apple tart
Prepare basic recipe, replacing cinnamon in filling with 1/4 teaspoon ground
cloves or ground nutmeg.

french apple tart with almond pastry
Prepare basic recipe, replacing 2 ounces flour in pastry with 1/2 cup
ground almonds.

french apple tart with apple compote
Prepare basic recipe, simmering 1 pound peeled, cored, and chopped cooking
apples with 3 tablespoons orange juice until soft enough to mash. Sweeten
apple compote with a little sugar to taste before spooning into pastry case
in an even layer and topping with sliced apples.

french apple tart with pecans
Prepare basic recipe, scattering 2 tablespoons chopped pecans (or toasted
slivered almonds) over glazed tart.

variations

kiwi, orange & white chocolate mille-feuilles

see base recipe page 100

kiwi, orange & dark chocolate mille-feuilles
Prepare basic recipe, replacing white chocolate with dark chocolate.

seared kiwi, orange & white chocolate party mille-feuille
Prepare basic recipe, dividing puff pastry into 3 equal blocks and rolling out each thinly to rectangles roughly 4 by 10 inches. Bake until golden brown without dusting with confectioners' sugar. When cool, dust 1 layer thickly with confectioners' sugar, heat a metal skewer until very hot, and mark a crisscross pattern in the sugar, reheating skewer as necessary. This will be the top layer. Stack the rectangles as in basic recipe, making 1 large mille-feuille.

kiwi, orange & dark chocolate mille-feuilles with hazelnuts
Prepare basic recipe, drizzling melted dark chocolate over top pieces of pastry before assembling. Scatter over chopped toasted hazelnuts to serve.

kiwi & orange mille-feuilles with vanilla cream
Prepare basic recipe, omitting white chocolate and using 1 cup cream, whipped with 1 teaspoon vanilla extract.

mixed fresh fruit mille-feuilles
Prepare basic recipe, using mixed fruits in filling.

variations

blackberry & apple oatmeal crumble

see base recipe page 102

blackberry, banana & apple oatmeal crumble
Prepare basic recipe, replacing 1/2 pound apples with 2 medium bananas
or 1 large one, peeled and sliced. Stir banana into cooked apples with
the blackberries.

blackberry & apple crumble with almond topping
For a less crunchy topping, replace chopped walnuts with ground almonds.

mixed summer fruit oatmeal crumble
Prepare basic recipe, replacing blackberries with mixed fruits such as pitted
cherries, raspberries, and blueberries.

blackberry & apple crumble with granola topping
Prepare basic recipe, replacing walnuts and oatmeal in topping with granola
(break up any large pieces) or muesli.

blackberry & apple oatmeal–raisin crumble
Prepare basic recipe, replacing half the walnuts in topping with raisins.

meringues & choux pastry desserts

Stunning additions to a buffet party table and guaranteed to draw gasps of delight from your guests every time — nothing can beat a crisp, cloudlike meringue or pile of cream-filled profiteroles when you're cooking to impress.

meringue gâteau with lemon curd filling

see variations page 129

Meringues make delicious desserts, but unless you're into whipping up your own mayonnaise or crème anglaise, it can be a problem working out what to do with the egg yolks. In this recipe, the yolks are turned into lemon curd for the filling.

for the meringue
4 large egg whites
3/4 cup (5 1/2 oz.) granulated sugar
2/3 cup (3 oz.) confectioners' sugar
1 tbsp. cornstarch

for the lemon curd
finely grated zest and juice of 4 lemons
4 large egg yolks
1/2 cup (4 oz.) unsalted butter, cut up
generous 1 cup (8 oz.) granulated sugar
extra confectioners' sugar, to dust

Draw two 7-inch squares on two sheets of nonstick baking parchment. Place sheets upside down on baking sheets. Preheat oven to 225°F. To make meringue, whisk egg whites until soft peak stage. Whisk in granulated sugar, a spoonful at a time, until mixture starts to thicken, then whisk in the rest in a slow, steady stream, continuing to whisk until thick and stiff. Sift in confectioners' sugar and cornstarch and fold in gently with a large metal spoon until just combined. Pipe or spread the meringue over the drawn squares on the baking parchment. Bake for about 3 hours until dry and crisp. Cool in the turned-off oven. To make lemon curd, whisk zest, juice, yolks, butter, and sugar in a large heatproof bowl. Place bowl over a pan of simmering water, and stir constantly until melted and thickened. Remove bowl from heat and let lemon curd cool, stirring occasionally. Chill until needed. Sandwich meringue layers with lemon curd and dust top with confectioners' sugar. Serve with fruit.

Serves 8

mango meringue pie

see variations page 130

Traditional lemon meringue pie is given an exotic new twist with a tangy layer of fragrant mango under the puffy white cloud of meringue.

for the pastry
2 cups (7 oz.) flour
7 tbsp. (3 1/2 oz.) unsalted butter, cut up
2–3 tbsp. chilled water
1 egg yolk

for the filling
2 very ripe mangoes
finely grated zest of 2 limes or 1 orange
for the topping
3 large egg whites
scant 1 cup (6 oz.) sugar

To make the pastry, sift flour into a bowl and rub in butter until the consistency is like bread crumbs. Mix in enough chilled water to make a smooth, soft dough. Wrap dough in plastic wrap and chill for 30 minutes.

Preheat oven to 375°F. Roll out pastry on a lightly floured surface and line an 8-inch flan pan, which is about 1 1/4 inches deep. Line pastry with waxed paper, fill with baking beans, and bake for 20 minutes. Remove beans and paper, brush base and sides of pastry with egg yolk, and return to oven for 5 minutes. Remove from oven and let cool. Reduce oven temperature to 300°F. To make the filling, peel, pit and chop mangoes. Mix with zest, and spoon into pastry shell. To make the topping, whisk egg whites until standing in soft peaks, then whisk in sugar, a tablespoon at a time, until whites are stiff and shiny. Spoon meringue over chopped mango, spreading it right to the edges so it forms a seal with pastry (you do not want juices to bubble out). Bake for 30 minutes or until meringue is golden and crisp. Let cool before serving.

Serves 6–8

cinnamon meringue slice layered with Caribbean fruits

see variations page 131

The meringue layers can be made ahead and stored in an airtight container and then assembled with the cream and fruit about 1-2 hours before serving.

for the meringue layers
3 large egg whites
4 1/2 tbsp. (2 oz.) light brown sugar
generous 1/2 cup (4 oz.) granulated sugar
1 1/2 tsp. cornstarch
1 1/2 tsp. white wine vinegar
1 tsp. ground cinnamon

for the filling
1 cup heavy cream
4 tbsp. coconut milk
about 1 lb. mixed tropical fruits (such as
papaya, figs, Cape gooseberries),
prepared as necessary and cut into pieces

Preheat oven to 225°F. Draw two rectangles measuring roughly 4x11 inches on a sheet of baking parchment. Place paper upside down on a baking sheet. To make the meringue layers, whisk egg whites until standing in soft peaks. Whisk in brown sugar, a couple of teaspoonfuls at a time, so it is evenly incorporated. Then whisk in granulated sugar in three equal batches, adding cornstarch, vinegar, and cinnamon with final batch. Pipe or spread meringue over the marked rectangles, dividing it equally. Bake for 2–2 1/2 hours or until pale golden and crisp. Let meringues cool in turned-off oven. When cooled completely, store in an airtight container. One or two hours before serving, make the filling. Whip cream and coconut milk together until stiff. Spread some coconut cream over one meringue layer and top with half the fruit. Top with more cream and put second meringue layer on top. Pipe or spoon remaining cream down the center and decorate with remaining fruit. Chill until ready to serve. To serve, cut into slices with a sharp serrated knife.
Serves 6

strawberry, kiwi & orange pavlova

see variations page 132

A favorite party dessert that will never fail to elicit whoops of delight from your guests. Once you've whisked up the egg white mixture for the meringue, dab tiny blobs of it in each corner of the baking sheet to stop the baking parchment sliding.

for the meringue
generous 1 cup (8 oz.) granulated sugar
1 tsp. lemon juice
4 large egg whites
1 tbsp. cornstarch

for the filling
scant 1 cup (7 oz.) heavy cream
heaping 1/2 cup (4 fl. oz.) sour cream
finely grated zest of 1 orange
9 oz. fresh strawberries, sliced
1 orange, peeled and segmented
2 kiwi fruit, peeled and sliced

Draw a 9-inch circle on a sheet of nonstick baking parchment, turn parchment over, and place it on a baking sheet. Preheat oven to 275°F. To make the meringue, put sugar, lemon juice, and 1 egg white in a large bowl. Whisk with electric beater on low speed until combined. Add another egg white, whisk for 2 minutes, then add remaining 2 whites and whisk for about 5 minutes on fast speed or until mixture is stiff and shiny. Finally, whisk in cornstarch. Spoon meringue onto parchment. Spread it out with a palette knife to fill the drawn circle, hollowing out the center a little. Bake for 1-1 1/2 hours, or until very pale golden and crisp on the outside but still soft in the middle. Turn off oven and leave meringue inside until it has cooled completely. No more than 1 hour before serving, make the filling. Whip cream, sour cream, and orange zest together until mixture just holds its shape. Place meringue on a serving plate and spoon cream over it, leaving a narrow border around the top. Pile sliced strawberries, orange segments, and kiwi slices over cream and serve.
Serves 6-8

choux ring with strawberries & blueberries

see variations page 133

You can pipe the choux onto the baking parchment or simply shape it with two spoons, but make sure the individual puffs are butted up close against each other.

for the choux ring
1 cup water
6 tbsp. (3 oz.) unsalted butter, cut up
1 1/3 cups (4 1/2 oz.) white bread flour, sifted
3 medium eggs, beaten
1 tbsp. granulated sugar

for the filling
4 tbsp. (2 oz.) granulated sugar
1 1/2 cups heavy cream
4 oz. fresh strawberries, hulled and sliced
4 oz. fresh blueberries
confectioners' sugar, to dust

Preheat oven to 400°F. Draw a 7-inch circle on a sheet of baking parchment and place it upside down on a greased baking sheet. To make the choux ring, heat water and butter in a pan until melted. Bring to a boil, remove from heat, and add flour. Beat briskly until mixture forms a smooth ball. Let cool slightly. Gradually beat in eggs, add the sugar with the last addition of egg. Not all the egg may be needed (although the paste should be smooth and shiny, it's important that it still holds its shape). Spoon or pipe mixture into mounds around the marked circle. Bake for 40 minutes or until golden brown. Remove, carefully split the ring in half horizontally through the center. Place halves split-side up on baking sheet and return to oven for 5 minutes. Cool on a wire rack. To make the filling, whip sugar and cream together until it just holds its shape. If the choux ring has become soft, recrisp it in a hot oven. Spoon half the whipped cream over the bottom half of the cold choux ring; top with berries and remaining cream. Set lid on top and dust with confectioners' sugar.
Serves 8–10

coffee meringue kisses

see variations page 134

These would make an attractive accompaniment to a bowl of fresh fruit or, if you decide not to serve a formal dessert, you could make mini versions and enjoy them with coffee or tea. The unfilled meringues can be made well ahead and stored in an airtight container.

for the meringues
3 large egg whites
scant 1 cup (6 oz.) sugar
1 tsp. coffee extract (or 1 tbsp. instant coffee
    dissolved in 1 tbsp. boiling water
    and cooled)

for the decoration & filling
6 oz. dark chocolate, chopped
1/2 cup heavy cream
1 tsp. vanilla extract
cocoa powder, to dust

Preheat oven to 225°F. Line two baking sheets with nonstick baking parchment. To make the meringues, whisk egg whites in a large bowl until soft peak stage. Whisk in sugar, 1 teaspoon at a time to begin with. Then, as egg whites start to thicken, add sugar in a steady stream. When all the sugar has been added, whisk in coffee. Spoon or pipe 12 mounds of meringue on each baking sheet. Bake for 2 hours or until dry and crisp. Allow to cool in the turned-off oven, then carefully lift meringues from parchment.

To decorate and make the filling, melt chocolate in a bowl set over a pan of hot water, stirring occasionally until smooth. Line baking sheets with clean parchment and dip bottoms of meringues in melted chocolate. Place them, chocolate-side down, on the parchment. Drizzle with remaining chocolate and let set. Whip cream with vanilla until it holds its shape. Use it to sandwich meringues together in pairs. Dust lightly with cocoa powder to serve.

Serves 12

almond & apricot meringue roulade

see variations page 135

Adding cornstarch and either lemon juice or vinegar to a meringue mixture keeps the center of the baked meringue marshmallow-soft and the outside crisp.

for the roulade
4 large egg whites
3/4 cup (5 1/2 oz.) sugar, plus extra for dusting
2 tsp. cornstarch
1 tsp. white wine vinegar or lemon juice
3 oz. blanched almonds, toasted and finely chopped or ground to a coarse powder

for the filling
7 fl. oz. crème fraîche
11 oz. fresh or canned apricot halves, chopped
confectioners' sugar, to dust

Grease and line a 9x13-inch jellyroll pan with nonstick baking parchment. Preheat oven to 325°F. To make the roulade, whisk egg whites to soft peaks. Gradually whisk in sugar until mixture is stiff and shiny. Add cornstarch and vinegar or lemon juice with the last of the sugar. Reserve 2 tablespoons almonds and fold the rest into meringue with a large metal spoon. Spoon mixture into prepared pan and spread out evenly to edges and corners. Scatter remaining almonds on top and bake for 25 minutes until pale golden and crisp. Lay a sheet of parchment on work surface and dust it with granulated sugar. Turn out meringue onto parchment, peel off lining paper, and leave until cold. To make the filling, spread crème fraîche over meringue, smoothing it out to the edges but leaving a border of about 1 inch down one long side. Scatter chopped apricots over crème fraîche and roll up from the long side where the cream has been spread right to the edge. Place roulade on a serving plate, seam down, and chill for 30 minutes. Dust with confectioners' sugar before serving.
Serves 6–8

crackle-topped profiteroles with orange cream

see variations page 136

If the choux balls go soft when cool, put them back on a baking sheet and return them to a hot oven for 5 minutes, which will recrisp them beautifully.

for the choux
scant 1 cup (3 oz.) white bread flour
1/2 cup water
4 tbsp. (2 oz.) unsalted butter, in small pieces
2 medium eggs, beaten
1 tsp. sugar
finely grated zest of 1 small orange

for the caramel
scant 1 cup (6 oz.) sugar
3 tbsp. water
for the filling
2 oranges
scant 1 cup (7 fl. oz.) heavy or whipping cream

Preheat oven to 400°F. Grease 2 baking sheets and line with baking parchment. To make the choux, sift flour onto a plate. Heat water and butter together in a pan over a low heat until butter has melted. Bring to a boil, remove from heat, and add the flour. Beat with a wooden spoon until mixture forms a smooth ball. Allow to cool a little, then beat in eggs, a little at a time, with the sugar. Pipe 18 small balls, well spaced apart, onto the baking sheets. Bake for 25 minutes, until crisp. Remove, pierce a hole in the side of each puff, and return to oven for 5 minutes. Cool puffs on a wire rack. To make the caramel, heat sugar and water and boil until sugar caramelizes and turns golden brown. Remove pan from heat and dip base of pan in a bowl of cold water. Using tongs, dip top of each puff into caramel, and set on a plate to cool and harden. If caramel hardens before you're finished, place pan over low heat to remelt. For the filling, grate the zest of 1 orange into a bowl, add cream, and whip. Peel and segment oranges. Split profiteroles and fill with the cream and orange segments to serve.
Serves 6

floating islands with passion fruit crème anglaise

see variations page 137

Warming the passion fruit seeds and pulp makes it easier to separate them, but if you don't object to the seeds, simply stir the seeds and pulp into the crème anglaise.

for the crème anglaise
3 passion fruit
4 large egg yolks
4 tbsp. (2 oz.) sugar
1 cup light cream

for the floating islands
2 large egg whites
heaping 1/2 cup (4 oz.) sugar
for the caramel
1/2 cup (3 1/2 oz.) sugar
2 tbsp. water
3 tbsp. toasted flaked almonds

To make crème anglaise, halve passion fruit and scoop seeds into a small bowl. Microwave for 30 seconds on full power, then strain to remove seeds. Whisk yolks and sugar together until pale and creamy. Heat cream until almost boiling. Stir cream into yolk mixture then return to pan. Stir over low heat without boiling until mixture coats the back of the spoon. Stir in passion fruit. To make floating islands, whisk egg whites to soft peaks. Gradually whisk in sugar until mixture is stiff and shiny. Half-fill a deep-frying pan or sauté pan with water and bring to a simmer. Spoon 6 small rounds of meringue into water and simmer over low heat for 2 minutes until they have doubled in size and feel firm, turning over once. Lift out meringues with a slotted spoon and drain on paper towels. Repeat with remaining mixture. To make caramel, dissolve sugar with water in a heavy pan and boil to a golden brown. Serve crème anglaise with meringues on top. Drizzle with hot caramel and sprinkle with almonds.
Serves 6

variations

meringue gâteau with lemon curd filling

see base recipe page 113

brown sugar meringue gâteau with lemon curd
Prepare basic recipe for meringue, substituting light brown sugar for granulated sugar and slowly whisking, rather than folding it in.

meringue gâteau with orange curd
Prepare basic recipe for lemon curd, replacing lemons with 2–3 oranges (depending on size). Or use 6 limes for lime curd.

meringue gâteau with fresh fruits & lemon curd
Prepare basic recipe, topping lemon curd with fresh fruit such as chopped peaches or strawberries, with passion fruit seeds and pulp spooned over, before adding top layer of meringue.

hazelnut meringue gâteau with lemon curd
Prepare basic recipe for meringue, folding in 2 tablespoons chopped hazelnuts at the end.

chocolate cream meringue gâteau
Prepare basic recipe, replacing lemon curd with chocolate cream. Melt 3 1/2 ounces chopped dark chocolate. Remove bowl from heat and stir in 1/2 cup crème fraîche. Let cool. Spread over meringue layer, top with raspberries and kiwi fruit slices, and add second layer.

variations

mango meringue pie

see base recipe page 114

mango meringue pie with cinnamon crumb crust
Prepare basic recipe, replacing pastry with a spicy graham cracker crust. Add 1/2 teaspoon pumpkin pie spice and 1 teaspoon ground cinnamon to graham cracker crumb mixture. Press over base and sides of flan pan and chill while preparing the filling.

peach meringue pie
Prepare basic recipe, replacing mangoes with 4–5 peeled and pitted ripe peaches (depending on size). Nectarines also work well.

mango chocolate chip meringue pie
Prepare basic recipe for meringue, folding 3 1/2 ounces small dark chocolate chips or finely chopped dark chocolate into whisked egg whites.

mango & ginger meringue pie
Prepare basic recipe, adding 1 tablespoon preserved ginger to mango flesh.

apple meringue pie
Prepare basic recipe, replacing mangoes with 4–5 apples. Peel, core, and chop apples, and simmer with the lime zest and juice and 3 tablespoons water until softened. Purée apples and their cooking juices before cooling and spooning into pastry shell.

variations

cinnamon meringue slice layered with Caribbean fruits

see base recipe page 117

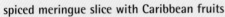

spiced meringue slice with Caribbean fruits
Prepare basic meringue, using 1 cup (8 ounces) granulated sugar. Replace cinnamon with 1/4 teaspoon grated nutmeg and 3/4 teaspoon pumpkin pie spice.

cinnamon meringue slice with orange cream
Prepare basic recipe, substituting an orange filling. Mix 2 tablespoons cornstarch with 1 tablespoon water. Stir in 4 large egg yolks, 3 1/2 ounces sugar, and grated zest and juice of 2 oranges. Bring 1/2 cup milk to a boil, pour onto yolk mixture, then whisk until thick and smooth. Let cool, then fold in 1/2 cup cream, whipped.

Christmas meringue slice
For a spectacular Christmas dessert, prepare basic recipe, using chestnut cream and winter fruits. Whip cream with 2 tablespoons chestnut purée and use fruits such as tangerine or clementine segments, figs, and poached cranberries.

pecan meringue slice with Caribbean fruits
Prepare basic recipe, folding 1 ounce coarsely ground pecans into meringue.

lemon mascarpone-filled meringue slice with Caribbean fruits
Prepare basic recipe, replacing coconut filling with 9 ounces mascarpone flavored with grated zest and juice of 2 lemons.

variations

strawberry, kiwi & orange pavlova

see base recipe page 118

chocolate-drizzled strawberry, kiwi & orange pavlova
Prepare basic recipe, drizzling baked meringue with 2 ounces melted dark chocolate and 2 ounces melted milk chocolate before filling.

golden fruits pavlova with coffee cream
Prepare basic recipe, replacing orange zest with 1 teaspoon coffee extract. Top with golden fruits, such as peaches, apricots and flaked almonds.

boozy strawberry & orange pavlova
Prepare basic recipe. Hull 1 pound strawberries, halving large ones, and macerate in 2 tablespoons fruit liqueur for 30 minutes. Fold three-quarters of strawberries into filling. Top pavlova with remaining strawberries.

pretty-in-pink pavlova
Prepare basic recipe, adding a few drops of pink food coloring to meringue mixture. Tint whipped cream, if you want, and top with fruits to match — strawberries and raspberries.

individual fruit & ice cream pavlovas
Prepare basic recipe, making individual pavlovas and filling with ice cream and fruit.

choux ring with strawberries & blueberries

see base recipe page 121

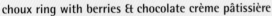

choux ring with berries & chocolate crème pâtissière
Prepare basic recipe, replacing whipped cream filling with chocolate crème pâtissière. Heat 1 cup whole milk with 1 ounce chopped dark chocolate until melted. Beat 2 large egg yolks with 2 ounces light brown sugar until creamy, stir in 2 tablespoons flour, then whisk in chocolate milk. Return to pan and stir over low heat until thickened. Dust top with sugar, cool and stir before using.

choux ring with lemon cream & lavender icing
Prepare basic recipe, adding finely grated zest of 1 lemon to whipping cream. Heat the juice of the lemon with 1 teaspoon culinary lavender, let stand for 30 minutes, then strain. Stir enough of the lavender-lemon juice into 5 1/2 ounces confectioners' sugar with a little violet food coloring and spread over the ring. Decorate with sprigs of lavender and berries such as blackberries and raspberries.

choux ring with berries & white chocolate drizzle
Prepare basic recipe, drizzling filled ring with 3 ounces melted white chocolate.

chocolate choux ring with berries
Prepare basic recipe for choux, replacing 1 tablespoon flour with 1 tablespoon cocoa powder.

variations

coffee meringue kisses

see base recipe page 122

coconut meringue kisses
Prepare basic recipe, omitting coffee flavoring from meringues and chocolate from whipped cream. Brush tops of cooked meringues with warmed apricot or strawberry jam and coat them in toasted flaked coconut. Sandwich in pairs with whipped cream and strawberry or apricot slices.

mocha hazelnut meringue kisses
Prepare basic recipe, dipping bases of the meringues first in melted dark chocolate and then in chopped toasted hazelnuts before sandwiching.

choc-n-orange meringue kisses with peppermint cream
Prepare basic recipe. Omit coffee flavoring and fold in 3 ounces finely chopped orange-flavored dark chocolate. Sandwich meringues with whipped cream flavored with 1 teaspoon peppermint extract instead of vanilla.

rainbow meringue kisses
Prepare basic recipe, replacing dark chocolate with white chocolate and tint with a few drops of your preferred food coloring. To serve, scatter over with sprinkles.

coffee & almond meringue kisses
Prepare basic recipe, folding 1 ounce ground almonds in meringue mixture.

almond & apricot meringue roulade

see base recipe page 124

raspberry & rosewater meringue roulade
Prepare basic recipe, adding 1 teaspoon rosewater to both the roulade mixture and the crème fraîche. Replace apricots with 9 ounces lightly crushed raspberries and the seeds of 1 pomegranate. Scatter crystallized rose petals over to serve.

macadamia & apricot meringue roulade
Prepare basic recipe, replacing ground almonds with toasted and coarsely ground macadamia nuts (or pecans).

peach & orange meringue roulade
Prepare basic recipe, adding finely grated zest of 1 orange to meringue mixture and filling roulade with mix of orange and peach pieces instead of apricots.

blueberry, cherry & lemon meringue roulade
Prepare basic recipe, replacing ground almonds in roulade with the finely grated zest of 1 lemon. Replace apricots in filling with equal quantities of blueberries and pitted cherries.

strawberry, pineapple & mascarpone meringue roulade
Prepare basic recipe, replacing crème fraîche with mascarpone, and apricots with equal quantities of chopped strawberries and pineapple pieces.

variations

crackle-topped profiteroles with orange cream

see base recipe page 127

orange cream profiteroles with dark chocolate sauce
Prepare basic recipe, omitting caramel. Serve with chocolate sauce (page 24).

orange cream choux pyramid with spun sugar
Prepare basic recipe, filling buns with orange cream by making a hole in the base and piping in the cream. Make the caramel with 9 ounces granulated sugar and 4 tablespoons water. Dip puffs into caramel and stack in a pyramid shape, sticking them together with the caramel. Return remaining caramel to heat, dip 2 forks in it, and flick strands of sugar over buns, repeating until pyramid is covered with fine threads.

crackle-topped profiteroles with pistachios and orange cream
Prepare basic recipe, sprinkling tops with chopped pistachios.

crackle-topped profiteroles with chocolate cream
Prepare basic recipe, replacing orange cream with whipped cream flavored with 1 tablespoon cocoa powder dissolved in 1 tablespoon hot water.

crackle-topped profiteroles filled with ice cream
Prepare basic recipe, replacing orange cream with small scoops of orange or another flavor ice cream.

variations

floating islands with passion fruit crème anglaise

see base recipe page 128

floating islands with raspberry crème anglaise
Prepare basic recipe, replacing passion fruit in crème anglaise with 4 ounces puréed and strained raspberries. Serve scattered with whole raspberries.

floating islands with fresh fruit & crème anglaise
Prepare basic recipe, adding a layer of fruit such as chopped banana, mango, sliced apricots, or kiwi fruit.

floating islands with pomegranate & pistachios
Prepare basic recipe, replacing passion fruit with 1 tablespoon grenadine. Replace almond topping with pomegranate seeds and chopped pistachios.

floating islands with chocolate crème anglaise
Prepare basic recipe, omitting passion fruit purée. Heat 2 ounces grated or chopped dark chocolate with the cream, stirring until melted, and use only 3 egg yolks.

floating islands with light coffee crème anglaise
For a less rich crème anglaise, prepare basic recipe, replacing cream with whole milk or mix of milk and cream. Instead of passion fruit purée, flavor crème anglaise with 1 teaspoon coffee extract or 2 tablespoons rum or brandy.

chilled desserts

From mastering the art of using gelatin to whipping

up a creamy zabaglione or caramelizing a brulée,

you'll find all you need to know — and plenty more —

in this chapter of delicious desserts to make ahead

and chill in the fridge.

coconut panna cotta with passion fruit coulis

see variations page 160

In Italian, panna cotta simply means "cooked cream" and the soft, silky texture of this famous dessert makes it a lovely finale to a special meal. The creams can be set in individual molds, turned out, and the coulis spooned around, or they can be served in glasses as they are here.

for the panna cotta
1 tbsp. unflavored gelatin
2 tbsp. cold water
1 cup heavy cream
1/2 cup coconut milk

5 1/2 oz. natural Greek yogurt
1/2 cup (3 ½ oz.) sugar
for the coulis
6 passion fruit, halved
1 1/2 cups freshly squeezed orange juice

To make the panna cotta, sprinkle gelatin over cold water and let soak for 5 minutes. Then set bowl in a pan of hot water, stirring until smooth and all granules have dissolved. Put cream, coconut milk, yogurt, and sugar in a pan. Heat gently until sugar melts and bubbles appear on surface. Remove pan from heat and stir in dissolved gelatin. Cool a little, then pour mixture into 6 glass dishes. Chill for several hours or overnight until set.

To make the coulis, scoop out passion fruit seeds and pulp into a small pan. Add orange juice, bring to a boil, and simmer for about 10 minutes until sauce reduces by about half. Push sauce through a sieve to remove seeds, and let cool. Spoon coulis over panna cotta and chill until ready to serve.

Serves 6

rum & ricotta pudding

see variations page 161

One of the simplest desserts, this is a wonderful way to enjoy really fresh, good-quality ricotta. It is very soft in texture, which makes it perfect for dunking biscotti.

1 lb. ricotta
scant 1/2 cup confectioners' sugar, sifted
4 tbsp. dark rum

1 tbsp. dessert wine, such as Marsala
  or Vinsanto
1 cup whipping cream, whipped until stiff

Mis together the ricotta, confectioners' sugar, and egg yolks until you have a thick, creamy texture. Stir in the rum and dessert wine, then fold in the whipped cream. Serve in chilled stemmed glasses, with biscotti for dunking. You can make this in advance and keep chiled until required, or whip it together quickly at the last moment.

Serves 6

blueberry muffin trifles

see variations page 162

Chill these for an hour or so before serving — they can also be made the day before and kept in the fridge overnight. Use a custard powder, available in large grocery stores, to make the custard, or use the recipe on pages 24–25.

4 blueberry muffins, cut into 1/2-inch pieces
9 oz. fresh blackberries or blackcurrants
2 tbsp. sugar
1/2 cup orange juice

8 oz. fresh blueberries
2 cups cold thick custard
4 oz. crème fraîche
2 tbsp. toasted flaked almonds

Divide muffins between 6 individual dishes or place in a large glass bowl. Put blackberries or blackcurrants in a pan, add sugar and orange juice, and simmer over low heat until fruit has softened. Purée in a blender or food processor and let cool before stirring in half the blueberries. Spoon all but 2 tablespoons of blueberry sauce over muffins.

Divide custard between dishes, spreading it in an even layer. Top with blobs of crème fraîche and remaining blueberry sauce. Scatter on almonds and remaining blueberries. Refrigerate until ready to serve.

Serves 6

il montebianco

see variations page 163

I have adapted this recipe from the more complicated and long-winded version that ends up with a mountain of cream, chestnut purée, and chocolate on a large platter. You'll need a potato ricer or mouli food mill to make this version.

1 lb. canned sweetened chestnut purée
4 tbsp. Strega liqueur (optional)
3 cups heavy or whipping cream
2 tbsp. sifted confectioners' sugar
1 tsp. vanilla extract
3 large ready-made meringues, crushed
3 oz. good-quality bittersweet chocolate
    (minimum cocoa solids content 70%), grated

1 tbsp. best-quality unsweetened powdered
    chocolate for dusting
1 1/2 tbsp. sifted confectioners' sugar
    for dusting
6 marrons glacés and 12 candied violets,
    to garnish

Mash the chestnut purée as much as possible to soften it, then mix with Strega if using. Set aside until required. Whip the cream, then sweeten with confectioners' sugar and flavor with vanilla extract. Fill the bottom of 6 stemmed glasses (martini glasses work best) with a little crushed meringue and cover with a layer of whipped cream. Push chestnut purée through a ricer or food mill onto whipped cream, then sprinkle with grated chocolate. Add another layer of purée and cover with whipped cream and chocolate as before. Add another layer of crushed meringues, then cover with a final layer of whipped cream. Allow a final small amount of chestnut purée to fall over the whipped cream, then sift the powdered chocolate and confectioners' sugar, mixed together, on top to dust lightly. Chill until required. Garnish with candied violets and marrons glacés before serving.

Serves 6

mango & mascarpone brûlées

see variations page 164

It's important to pick out a ripe mango, because if it's still hard it will also be tasteless, and have no sweet aroma, resulting in a disappointing dessert rather than one that is lush and fragrant.

1 ripe mango
6 large egg yolks
4 tbsp. (2 oz.) granulated sugar
4 oz. mascarpone cheese

1 1/2 cups light cream
1/2 tsp. vanilla extract
4 tbsp. light brown sugar

Peel mango and cut flesh away from pit. Chop flesh into small pieces or purée in food processor. Spoon into 6 medium-size ramekins or other heatproof dishes.

Beat together egg yolks and sugar until sugar has dissolved and mixture is light and creamy. Heat mascarpone and cream gently over low heat, stirring occasionally to combine, until bubbles begin to appear on surface. Pour onto yolk mixture, add vanilla, and stir well to combine. Strain custard into ramekins and place them in a roasting pan. Pour hot water into pan to come about 1 inch up sides of ramekins.

Preheat oven to 300°F. Bake custards for 30–35 minutes or until just set. Remove from roasting pan and let cool, then chill for several hours. About 1 hour before serving, spoon brown sugar evenly over custards, completely covering the top. Caramelize in oven under broiler or use a cook's blowtorch until sugar is a rich dark brown and crisp. Let cool so topping hardens.

Serves 6

tiramisu with pears

see variations page 165

A fruity variation on the Italian specialty that has become one of the world's favorite desserts. If you prefer, it can be made in one large dish, and if children are in the party, omit the liqueur.

4 oz. ladyfingers, coarsely chopped
1/2 cup cold strong black coffee
2 tbsp. Tia Maria or Kahlua liqueur
1–2 ripe pears (depending on size), peeled,
    cored, and chopped or sliced

7 tbsp. (3 oz.) sugar
18 oz. mascarpone cheese
1 tsp. unsweetened cocoa powder

Place some of the chopped ladyfingers in bottom of 4 dessert dishes. Mix coffee and liqueur together and spoon a little over ladyfingers.

Stir three-quarters of the pears into mascarpone with the sugar, then spoon a layer into each dish. Continue layering ladyfingers, coffee, and mascarpone mixture in dishes, finishing with a mascarpone layer. Chill until ready to serve.

Just before serving top each tiramisu with a few pear slices and dust with cocoa.

Serves 4

cappuccino whips

see variations page 166

You can buy custard or make your own (pages 24–25) for these creamy treats. The custard should have the consistency of unwhipped heavy cream, or what the French call crème anglaise.

1/2 cup heavy cream
1 cup pouring custard
2 tbsp. espresso or strong black coffee

5 1/2 oz. milk chocolate, chopped
extra whipped cream and grated dark chocolate,
    to decorate

Heat cream, custard, and coffee together until almost boiling. Remove pan from heat and add chopped chocolate, stirring until chocolate melts. Cool and leave until starting to thicken, stirring occasionally. Then, spoon into small cups or glasses and chill for 2–3 hours to firm. To serve, top with a spoonful of whipped cream and sprinkle with grated chocolate.

Serves 4

apricot, honey & ricotta mousse

see variations page 167

When they're in season, use fresh apricots rather than canned to make the mousse, topping off the liquid to make the gelatin with extra apple juice.

1 (14 1/2-oz.) can apricot halves in fruit juice
2 tbsp. honey
9 oz. ricotta cheese
1/2 cup heavy cream
1 package lemon gelatin

to decorate
6 tbsp. heavy cream or Greek yogurt
3 tbsp. toasted chopped nuts
6 tsp. honey

Drain apricot halves, reserving juice and two halves for decoration. Put remaining apricots in a food processor or blender, and add honey and ricotta. Blend together until smooth. In a large bowl, whisk cream until thick. Add apricot mixture and stir until evenly mixed. Make the lemon gelatin according to package instructions, but use only 1 1/2 cups liquid. Use enough boiling water to dissolve the gelatin, then top off with juice from apricot can. Set aside until gelatin starts to thicken. Gradually stir apricot mixture into thickened gelatin. Spoon into stemmed glasses or serving dishes and chill until set.

Decorate each mousse with a spoonful of heavy cream or Greek yogurt, a scattering of chopped nuts, and chopped reserved apricot halves. Drizzle with honey.

Serves 6

rhubarb fool

see variations page 168

The slim young stalks of early rhubarb are vivid pink in color, so they give desserts such as this creamy fool a real lift. Later rhubarb tends to be greener, so a dash of pink food coloring might be needed to provide the necessary eye appeal. You can make this in the morning and let it chill all day, if you like.

1 lb. fresh rhubarb
1/2 cup (4 oz.) light brown sugar
juice of 1 lemon
1 tbsp. custard powder (available in
  supermarkets)

1/2 cup milk
pink food coloring (optional)
1/2 cup whipping cream
crushed gingersnaps, to decorate

Preheat oven to 350°F. Cut rhubarb stalks into 2-inch lengths, place in a bowl, and mix with sugar and lemon juice. Pour rhubarb into a shallow baking pan, spread out evenly, and bake for 10 minutes. Allow to cool and then purée in a food processor or blender.

Mix custard powder with a little milk. Heat remaining milk in a small pan until almost boiling, pour onto custard powder, and stir until mixed. Return pan to low heat and stir until custard is smooth and thickened. Whisk custard into puréed rhubarb, add a little pink food coloring if necessary, and let cool. Whip cream until standing in soft peaks. Fold three-quarters of the whipped cream into rhubarb custard and spoon into serving glasses or dishes. Divide remaining cream between dishes and swirl in with a skewer. Chill until ready to serve. Serve decorated with a sprinkling of crushed gingersnaps.

Serves 4

sparkling clementine jello

see variations page 169

A pretty party dessert that's low in calories if you go easy on the cream, or replace it with reduced-fat crème fraîche or yogurt.

1 1/2 tbsp. unflavored gelatin
3 tbsp. cold water
13 fl. oz. (1/2 bottle) dry pink champagne or
    sparkling wine

few drops of pink food coloring (optional)
1 tbsp. sugar
4 clementines
whipped cream, to serve

Soak gelatin in the cold water for 5 minutes to soften, then dissolve by setting the bowl in a pan of hot water. Pour about one-third of the champagne or sparkling wine into a small pan. Add gelatin and sugar, and heat gently until sugar dissolves. Remove from heat and pour into a measuring cup or small pitcher. Top off with remaining champagne or wine, adding a few drops of food coloring if desired.

Peel clementines, pull away any loose pith, and with a sharp knife, slice a couple of pieces of zest into fine strips. Keep in a small bowl of cold water until needed. Divide half the clementine slices between 4 stemmed wine or cocktail glasses and pour in enough of the champagne mixture to cover them. Chill until just set, add remaining clementine slices (reserving a few for decoration), and then carefully pour remaining mixture into glasses. Chill again until firmly set. Top each jelly with a spoonful of whipped cream, reserved clementine slices, and a few strips of zest.

Serves 4

orange zabaglione with chocolate cake pops

see variations page 170

Warm zabaglione is a delicious dessert, but it does involve lots of last minute whipping — time you'd probably rather spend chatting to your guests. This version can be made ahead and chilled until needed.

for the zabaglione
4 large egg yolks
finely grated zest of 2 oranges
1/2 cup (3 1/2 oz.) granulated sugar
6 1/2 tbsp. Marsala
for the chocolate cake pops
1 cup (3 1/2 oz.) plain sponge cake crumbs

2 tsp. dark brown sugar
2 oz. dark chocolate, melted
4 tbsp. (2 oz.) unsalted butter, melted
8 oz. milk or white chocolate, melted
chocolate sprinkles or other small
    edible decorations

To make the zabaglione, put egg yolks, half the orange zest, and sugar in a large bowl, and whisk together until foamy. Add Marsala and whisk again briefly. Set bowl over a pan of simmering water, making sure bottom of bowl doesn't touch water, and whisk until mixture becomes thick and creamy. Spoon into 4 dessert glasses or dishes and chill for at least 1 hour or until ready to serve. To make the chocolate cake pops, put cake crumbs in a bowl and stir in sugar, melted dark chocolate, and butter. Knead mixture together and shape into 8 small balls. Chill until firm. Dip balls in melted milk or white chocolate, scatter chocolate sprinkles over them, and put on a plate or baking sheet lined with foil. Leave in a cool place (not the fridge) until chocolate has set. Push a plastic lollipop stick into each, making a small hole in the chocolate shell with the point of a sharp knife, if necessary. Serve with zabaglione.
Serves 4

mango & lime mousse

see variations page 171

Sweet, aromatic mangoes are a real taste of the tropics, but, as with all exotic fruits, it's good to use your nose before you buy. If a mango has a honeyed, fragrant aroma, the chances are it will taste good too. No scent usually means no flavor either.

1 tbsp. unflavored gelatin
2 tbsp. cold water
2–3 mangoes (total weight of prepared flesh about 1 lb.)
finely grated zest and juice of 2 limes

3/4 cup heavy cream
1 large egg white
4 tbsp. (2 oz.) light brown sugar
extra whipped cream and shreds of lime zest, to decorate

In a small bowl, soak gelatin in the cold water for 5 minutes. Set bowl in a pan of hot water and leave until gelatin has dissolved.

Peel mangoes and cut flesh away from fibrous pit. Chop flesh coarsely and place in a food processor or blender with lime zest and juice. Blend to a purée. Stir in dissolved gelatin.

Whip cream until it just holds its shape and fold into mango mixture. Whisk egg white until standing in soft peaks, then gradually whisk in sugar. Stir 1 tablespoon whisked egg white into mango mixture and then gently fold in the rest. Spoon into serving dishes and chill for 2–3 hours until set. Decorate each mousse with a spoonful of whipped cream and a few fine shreds of lime zest.

Serves 6

variations

coconut panna cotta with passion fruit coulis

see base recipe page 139

orange panna cotta with passion fruit coulis
Prepare basic recipe, replacing coconut milk with whole milk and adding finely grated zest of 1 orange to cream mixture.

coconut panna cotta with mango coulis
Prepare basic recipe, replacing passion fruit coulis with mango coulis. Purée flesh of 1 ripe mango with enough exotic fruit juice to make smooth sauce.

chocolate panna cotta with passion fruit coulis
Prepare basic recipe, replacing coconut milk with light cream and adding 2 teaspoons cocoa powder, dissolved in 1 tablespoon hot water.

coffee panna cotta with crunchy hazelnut topping
Prepare basic recipe, replacing coconut milk with cold black coffee. Sprinkle chilled panna cotta with chopped toasted hazelnuts and chocolate-covered coffee beans.

berry smoothie panna cotta
Prepare basic recipe, replacing coconut milk with a strawberry or blueberry smoothie. Top with strawberry or blueberry coulis, made by puréeing 9 ounces strawberries or blueberries with enough apple or orange juice to make a smooth sauce (about 3/4 cup).

rum & ricotta pudding

see base recipe page 140

rum and ricotta pudding with toasted almonds
Prepare the basic recipe, adding 3 tablespoons slivered toasted almonds along with the rum and dessert wine. Sprinkle the top of each serving with a few more almonds.

coffee ricotta pudding
Prepare basic recipe, replacing the dark rum with the same amount of strong espresso coffee. Garnish each serving with a coffee bean.

limoncello & ricotta pudding
Prepare the basic recipe, adding the grated zest of 1 lemon, and replacing the rum and dessert wine with 5 tablespoons limoncello liqueur.

amaretti & ricotta pudding
Prepare the basic recipe, crumbling in 6 amaretti cookies into the mixture before folding in the whipped cream. Serve with amaretti cookies for dunking.

variations

blueberry muffin trifles

see base recipe page 142

raspberry muffin trifles
Prepare basic recipe, using raspberry muffins and raspberries instead of
blueberries. Replace blackberries or black currants in purée with strawberries.

blueberry muffin trifles with vanilla sauce
Prepare basic recipe, replacing custard with vanilla cream sauce. Mix 3 large
egg yolks with 3 ounces confectioners' sugar, 1 1/2 tbsp. cornstarch, and
2 tablespoons milk until smooth. Heat remaining milk with 1/2 cup light
cream until almost boiling, whisk into egg mixture, then return to pan and
stir over a low heat until thick and smooth. Stir in 1 teaspoon vanilla extract
and cool before spooning over muffins and fruit purée.

blueberry muffin trifles with whipped cream & amaretti
Prepare basic recipe, topping trifles with spoonfuls of whipped cream and
scattering crushed amaretti over them with the blueberries.

variations

il montebianco

see base recipe page 145

montebianco al cioccolato bianco
Prepare basic recipe, replacing the chocolate with grated white chocolate
and the powdered chocolate with melted white chocolate.

montebianco al gianduja
Prepare basic recipe, replacing the grated chocolate with grated gianduja
chocolate and the powdered chocolate with melted gianduja.

montebianco al Strega
Prepare basic recipe, replacing the brandy with Strega liqueur.

variations

mango & mascarpone brûlées

see base recipe page 146

peach & mascarpone brûlées
Prepare basic recipe, replacing mango with 2–3 ripe peaches, depending on size, peeled and pitted.

mango & crème fraîche brûlées
Prepare basic recipe, replacing mascarpone with crème fraîche.

apricot, almond & mascarpone brûlées
Prepare basic recipe, replacing mango with 4 large pitted apricots, puréeing them with 2 tablespoons amaretto liqueur or a few drops of almond extract.

mango & chocolate brûlées
Prepare basic recipe, whisking 1 tablespoon cocoa powder, dissolved in 1 tablespoon hot water and cooled, with egg yolks and sugar.

blueberry brûlées
Prepare basic recipe, replacing mango with 6 ounces fresh blueberries, roughly chopped (not puréed) and divided between ramekins.

variations

tiramisu with pears

see base recipe page 148

ginger tiramisu with pears
Prepare basic recipe, replacing ladyfingers with gingerbread, broken into
small pieces.

tiramisu with nectarines
Prepare basic recipe, replacing pears with 1–2 nectarines, depending on size,
pitted and chopped.

pear & orange tiramisu
Prepare basic recipe, stirring 1 teaspoon finely grated orange zest into
mascarpone with chopped pears.

tiramisu with pears & grappa
Prepare basic recipe, replacing coffee liqueur with the Italian brandy, grappa.

tiramisu with grapes
Prepare basic recipe, replacing pears with 5 ounces seedless green grapes,
halved or roughly chopped.

variations

cappuccino whips

see base recipe page 150

mocha whips
Prepare basic recipe, replacing milk chocolate with dark chocolate.

boozy cappuccino whips
Prepare basic recipe, stirring 2 tablespoons coffee liqueur into cream mixture after adding the chocolate.

white cappuccino whips
Prepare basic recipe, replacing milk chocolate with white chocolate and stirring in 1/2 teaspoon vanilla extract after chocolate has melted.

pear & cappuccino whips
Prepare basic recipe, adding a chopped pear half to each serving cup or glass before spooning in the whip.

orange cappuccino whips
Prepare basic recipe, adding 1 teaspoon finely grated orange zest to cream, custard, and coffee mixture before heating.

variations

apricot, honey & ricotta mousse

see base recipe page 152

peach, honey & ricotta mousse
Prepare basic recipe, substituting 1 (14 1/2-oz.) can peach halves in fruit juice for
apricots. Reserve only one peach half for decoration.

apricot, maple & ricotta mousse
Prepare basic recipe, replacing honey with 3 tablespoons maple syrup when
making mousse and drizzling extra syrup over for decoration.

apricot, honey & yogurt mousse
Prepare basic recipe, replacing 4 ounces of ricotta with natural Greek yogurt.

apricot, orange and ricotta mousse
Prepare basic recipe, replacing apple juice with orange juice.

apricot, honey & yogurt mousse with blueberry topping
Prepare basic recipe, replacing cream or yogurt topping with blueberry compote.
Simmer 11 ounces blueberries with 1/2 cup orange juice in a covered pan until
blueberries are soft. Mix 2 teaspoons arrowroot with 2 tablespoons cold water
and stir into berries. Heat gently until sauce thickens, stirring occasionally. Let
cool, then spoon some compote over each mousse.

variations

rhubarb fool

see base recipe page 153

blackberry fool
Prepare basic recipe, replacing rhubarb with 1 pound blackberries and
omitting lemon juice. Simmer blackberries with 1/2 cup orange juice until
soft, then blend in a food processor. Push mixture through a sieve and
discard seeds. Stir in 2 tablespoons light brown sugar.

plum & cardamom fool
Prepare basic recipe, replacing rhubarb with 1 1/2 pounds red plums, halved
and pitted, and adding 1 teaspoon ground cardamom before baking.

rhubarb & yogurt fool
Prepare basic recipe, replacing whipping cream with natural Greek yogurt.

raspberry fool
Prepare basic recipe, replacing rhubarb with 12 ounces raspberries. Crush
lightly with a fork, sprinkle with 2 tablespoons light brown sugar and the
lemon juice, and set aside. Fold raspberries into custard with their juice,
before adding whipped cream.

variations

sparkling clementine jello

see base recipe page 154

rosé clementine jellies
Prepare basic recipe, replacing pink champagne with a dry rosé wine such as one from Chile or the south of France.

sparkling apple & raspberry jellies
Prepare basic recipe, replacing pink champagne with clear sparkling apple juice and the clementines with 8 ounces raspberries. As apple juice is naturally sweet, the sugar can probably be omitted but taste the jelly if you're unsure.

port, cranberry & cherry jellies
Prepare basic recipe, replacing pink champagne with 3 fl. oz. ruby port and 1 cup cranberry juice (or use all cranberry juice) and the clementines with 8 ounces pitted black or red cherries.

sparkling bellini jellies
Prepare basic recipe, replacing pink champagne with Italian Prosecco (sparkling wine) and clementines with 2 ripe peaches, peeled, pitted, and chopped.

variations

orange zabaglione with chocolate cake pops

see base recipe page 156

orange zabaglione with chocolate drizzle
Prepare basic recipe, omitting cake pops. Melt 3 1/2 ounces dark chocolate with 4 tablespoons heavy cream. Cool and drizzle over zabaglione to serve.

orange zabaglione with orange slices & caramelized orange zest
Prepare basic recipe. Peel 2 large oranges, cut away pith, and divide into segments. Place in glasses before adding zabaglione. Decorate each glass with caramelized orange zest. Simmer fine strips of zest in a sugar syrup made with 1/2 cup water and 3 1/2 ounces confectioners' sugar for 10 minutes until syrup reduces by about half. Cool zest in syrup.

warm orange zabaglione with chocolate cake pops
Prepare basic recipe, serving zabaglione immediately while still warm.

orange zabaglione with ginger cake pops
Prepare basic recipe, replacing plain sponge cake crumbs with gingerbread crumbs in the cake pops.

lemon zabaglione with chocolate cake pops
Prepare basic recipe, replacing orange zest with the zest of 2 lemons.

mango & lime mousse

see base recipe page 158

lychee & strawberry mousse
Prepare basic recipe, replacing mangoes with 1 pound peeled and pitted lychees
and hulled strawberries (prepared total weight).

peach & orange mousse
Prepare basic recipe, replacing mangoes with 1 pound peeled and pitted peaches
(prepared weight). Replace lime zest and juice with grated zest and juice of
1 small orange.

mango & rum mousse
Prepare basic recipe, adding 2 tablespoons white or gold rum to whipped cream.

mango & coconut mousse
Prepare basic recipe, replacing cream with thick coconut milk (no need to whip it)
and folding this into the mango mixture.

mango & ginger mousse
Prepare basic recipe, sprinkling the top of each mousse with crushed gingersnaps.

frozen treats

A sophisticated strawberry smifreddo, creamy and
tangy limoncello ice cream, exotic coconut Malibu
Alaska, and a palate-cleansing pomegranate and
lychee granita are just a few of the frozen delights
you'll find in this chapter.

strawberry semifreddo

see variations page 194

An impressive but easy dessert that tastes as good as it looks. As vanilla is quite sweet, the sharp flavor of the strawberries provides a good contrast.

18 oz stawberries
3 eggs
2 egg yolks
1 tsp. vanilla extract
1 cup superfine sugar

1 2/3 cups cream
1/4 cup confectioners' sugar
2 tsp. lemon juice
redcurrants, to decorate

Line a 5 1/2 x 9-inch loaf tin with plastic wrap. Reserve 2 strawberries for the decoration. Crush the remaining strawberries with a potato masher to make a chunky puree. Put the eggs, egg yolks, vanilla, and superfine sugar in a heatproof bowl, place over a pan of simmering (not boiling) water and whisk with an electric whisk for 4 minutes. Remove from the heat and whisk until thick, frothy, and completely cool. Whisk the cream until thick and fold into the egg mixture. Spoon the mixture into the tin. Drizzle over half the strawberry puree and pass the handle of a wooden spoon through the mixture to produce a lightly marbled effect. Smooth the surface, cover with plastic wrap and freeze for at least 6 hours or overnight if possible.

Press the remaining puree through a fine sieve into a bowl. Stir in the icing sugar and lemon juice. Turn the semifreddo out of the tin on to a serving plate and peel away the plastic wrap. Drizzle with a little strawberry puree. Put the remaining strawberry puree into a small bowl. Decorate with redcurrants and the reserved strawberries. Cut into slices using a warmed knife and serve drizzled with strawberry puree.

Serves 6

coconut malibu alaska

see variations page 195

Store-bought vanilla ice cream is used to make this crunchy-topped dessert, so choose a good quality one that isn't soft scoop, which would melt too quickly in the oven.

1 1/4 pints vanilla ice cream, softened
1 large ripe mango or small papaya, peeled
    and chopped
2 tbsp. Malibu coconut liqueur

4 egg whites
scant 1 cup (6 oz.) sugar
1/2 lb. gingerbread, sliced
2 tbsp. unsweetened flaked coconut

Line a 2-lb. loaf pan with a double thickness of plastic wrap, letting it overhang the sides. Spoon ice cream into pan, packing it down firmly and hollowing out the middle. Puree the mango or papaya with the coconut liqueur and spoon into hollow. Fold plastic wrap over the top to cover and return to freezer until ready to serve. Before serving, preheat oven to its hottest setting. Whisk egg whites until standing in soft peaks, then gradually whisk in sugar until stiff.

Peel back plastic wrap from mango and ice cream and cover the top with gingerbread slices, pressing them down lightly. Invert onto a baking pan and unmold. Pull off plastic wrap and cover dessert with the meringue, spreading it over top and sides with a palette knife and creating a seal around the bottom. Sprinkle with coconut and bake for 5 minutes or until golden brown. Serve at once, cut into slices.

Serves 6

blackberry & mint parfait with amaretti

see variations page 196

Mint is a deliciously refreshing herb and one of the most versatile, as it's equally at home in savory dishes as sweet dishes. In this creamy parfait, it partners with blackberries to make a lovely summertime dessert. You can make your own sauce by using the recipe for raspberry coulis (page 24) and substituting blackberries for the raspberries, or buy a ready-made blackberry sauce.

12 oz. fresh blackberries
6 fresh mint leaves, roughly torn
scant 1 cup (4 oz.) confectioners' sugar
1 tbsp. lemon juice
1 cup heavy cream

1/2 cup light cream
4 oz. amaretti biscuits, crushed
blackberry dessert sauce, to serve
extra blackberries and mint leaves, to serve

Purée blackberries in a food processor or blender with mint leaves, confectioners' sugar, and lemon juice. In a bowl, whip creams together until thick, then fold in blackberry purée. Spoon into eight 4-oz. cups or molds (you could use empty yogurt containers), cover tops with foil, and freeze until solid. Transfer parfaits to fridge about 20 minutes before serving. Turn out onto serving plates and sprinkle with crushed amaretti. Serve with blackberry dessert sauce and garnish with extra blackberries and mint leaves.

Serves 8

brown bread & hazelnut ice cream

see variations page 197

An excellent recipe for using up leftover bread. The ice cream can be served on its own or with fresh fruit such as strawberries or black cherries.

scant 2 cups (4 oz.) fresh whole wheat
    bread crumbs
1/2 cup (2 oz.) finely chopped hazelnuts
4 1/2 tbsp. (2 oz.) light brown sugar
1/2 tsp. ground cinnamon
1 cup heavy cream

1/2 cup light cream
3 tbsp. golden rum
7 tbsp. (2 oz.) confectioners' sugar
chocolate sauce (recipe page 24) and toasted
    coarsely chopped hazelnuts, to serve

Preheat oven to 400°F. In a bowl, mix bread crumbs, hazelnuts, brown sugar, and cinnamon. Spread out evenly on a baking sheet. Bake for about 10 minutes, turning mixture over occasionally, until sugar has caramelized, crumbs are crisp, and hazelnuts are toasted. Let cool completely, then break up into small pieces with a rolling pin. Set aside.

Whisk creams together with rum in a bowl until they hold their shape. Sift in confectioners' sugar and fold in with a metal spoon. Transfer mixture to a freezer container and freeze for 2–3 hours or until slushy. Remove from freezer, tip into a bowl, and whisk to break up any ice crystals. Stir in crumb mixture and return to freezer container. Cover and freeze for several hours or overnight until firm. About 20 minutes before serving, transfer ice cream to fridge so it has time to soften. Serve ice cream in scoops topped with chocolate sauce and a scattering of toasted chopped hazelnuts.

Serves 4

espresso & almond praline semifreddo

see variations page 198

Neither a mousse nor an ice cream, this semifrozen Italian dessert falls somewhere in between. Made with cream and eggs, semifreddo translates as "half cold." This needs to be eaten quickly after serving, before it melts.

1/4 cup (2 oz.) blanched almonds
2/3 cup (5 oz.) light brown sugar, plus 4 tbsp. (2 oz.)
2 tbsp. instant espresso coffee granules
7 tbsp. hot water

2 tbsp. amaretto liqueur
3 large egg yolks
1 cup heavy cream
2 tbsp. toasted chopped almonds

Grease a baking sheet or line it with parchment. Put almonds and 4 tablespoons sugar in a small heavy pan and heat gently until sugar melts, stirring occasionally. Cook until sugar caramelizes and turns golden brown, then immediately tip almonds and caramel onto prepared baking sheet and leave until cold and hard. Grind almond praline to a coarse powder in food processor. Line bases of six 4-ounce molds or cups with waxed paper. Stir coffee into hot water until it dissolves. Cool slightly before stirring in liqueur. Let cool completely. In a large bowl, whisk together egg yolks and remaining sugar until pale and creamy. Gradually whisk in cold coffee. Whip cream until just holding its shape and fold in with almond praline until evenly combined. Spoon mixture into molds, cover with foil, and freeze for 8 hours or overnight. To serve, turn out onto dessert plates and peel off lining paper. Sprinkle with chopped almonds and serve immediately.

Serves 6

vanilla ice cream with black cherry compote

see variations page 199

For flavoring ice cream, a vanilla pod is much better than vanilla extract, as extracts tend to deteriorate during the freezing process and lose their flavor.

for the ice cream
1 cup light cream
1 vanilla pod
4 large egg yolks
generous 1/2 cup (4 oz.) sugar

1 cup heavy cream
for the black cherry compote
1 lb. fresh black cherries, pitted
1 3/4 cups sugar

To make ice cream, pour light cream into a heavy saucepan. Split vanilla pod lengthwise and scrape seeds into pan. In a bowl, mix egg yolks and sugar together. Heat cream until it comes to a boil and then slowly pour it into egg mixture, stirring constantly with a wooden spoon. Return mixture to pan and stir over low heat until it coats the back of the spoon. Do not let it boil. Pour into a bowl and set aside until completely cool, stirring occasionally. Beat heavy cream until thick, then fold into custard mixture. Pour mixture into a freezer container and freeze until partially frozen. Scrape out mixture into a chilled bowl and whisk until smooth. Return to freezer, cover, and freeze until solid. To make compote, heat cherries gently in a saucepan sprinkled with sugar until juice runs from cherries and sugar dissolves. Transfer ice cream from freezer to fridge about 30 minutes before serving to give it time to soften. Serve with warm or cold cherry compote spooned on top.

Serves 6

limoncello ice cream

see variations page 200

Adding liqueur to ice cream gives it a softer texture and avoids the necessity of beating the freezing mixture two or three times to break up ice crystals (the alcohol in the liqueur acts like antifreeze in a car).

3 large lemons
2/3 cup (3 oz.) confectioners' sugar

1 cup plus 2 tbsp. heavy cream
7 tbsp. limoncello

Using a vegetable peeler, shave zest from lemons in long strips. Squeeze lemon juice into a bowl and stir in sugar until dissolved. Add strips of zest and set aside in a cool place to macerate for 30 minutes or longer. Remove zest and discard. Add cream and limoncello to bowl and whip until mixture just holds its shape.

Transfer to a freezer container, cover, and freeze for several hours or overnight until solid. Transfer container to fridge about 15 minutes before serving to make it easier to form into scoops.

Serves 6

peach melba yogurt ice

see variations page 201

Both the creamy peach ice and raspberry water ice make great family desserts.

for the peach ice
6 fresh peaches, total weight 1 1/2 lbs.
juice of 1 lemon
3 large egg yolks
3/4 cup (5 1/2 oz.) sugar
1/2 cup milk
5 1/2 oz. natural Greek yogurt
for the raspberry ice
1 lb. fresh raspberries

3/4 cup (5 1/2 oz.) sugar
scant 1 cup water
juice of 1 lemon
juice of 1 orange
2 large egg whites
to serve
extra raspberries and small peach slices
raspberry coulis (page 24)

To make peach ice, put peaches in a bowl, cover with boiling water, leave for 1 minute, and drain. Peel and pit. Purée peach flesh with lemon juice. Whisk together yolks and sugar until creamy. Heat milk gently until it comes to a boil, then whisk into yolk mixture. Pour back into pan and stir over low heat until custard thickens. Remove from heat and let cool. Fold peach purée and yogurt into custard, pour into freezer container, and cover. To make raspberry ice, sprinkle raspberries with 2 tablespoons sugar. Let stand for 30 minutes, then blend, strain, and discard seeds. Heat remaining sugar and water, bring to a boil, and simmer 5 minutes. Remove from heat and stir in raspberry purée, lemon, and orange juices. Pour into freezer container and cover. Freeze both ices until firm around edges. Whisk, return to freezer for 1 hour, then whisk again. Whisk egg whites until stiff and gradually mix with partially frozen raspberry mixture. Return to freezer for 1 hour, then whisk again. Fill freezer container with alternate scoops of each ice. Swirl together and freeze. Transfer to refrigerator 30 minutes before serving in scoops topped with raspberries, peach slices, and raspberry coulis.
Serves 8–10

pomegranate & lychee granita

see variations page 202

A granita is similar to a sorbet, but while a sorbet has a smooth, silky texture, a granita is rougher and formed of large ice crystals made by breaking up the frozen mixture with a fork. Two contrasting colored granitas made with different fruits make a pretty and eye-catching dessert when layered in glasses.

for the pomegranate granita
1 1/2 cups pomegranate juice drink
7 tbsp. (3 oz.) sugar
for the lychee granita
8 oz. fresh lychees

7 tbsp. (3 oz.) sugar
1 cup water
to decorate
pomegranate seeds and peeled lychees

To make pomegranate granita, heat pomegranate juice and sugar gently until sugar dissolves. Set aside until cold, then pour into a freezer container. To make lychee granita, peel lychees and remove pits. In a food processor or blender, purée with sugar. Add water and blend briefly until mixed in. Strain purée into a freezer container.

Freeze both containers of granitas for about 2 hours or until partially frozen. Beat with a fork to mash unfrozen and frozen parts together until slushy. Return granitas to freezer for 1 hour, then break up with a fork again. Cover and return to freezer until needed. Transfer containers from freezer to fridge about 30 minutes before serving. Break up with a fork again to give a coarse texture and layer in dessert glasses. Serve topped with a few pomegranate seeds and peeled lychees.

Serves 8

blackcurrant sorbet

see variations page 203

In Victorian times, a "sorbet" always contained alcohol, arriving on the smartest dinner tables in the guise of frozen rum punches or claret cups. In the twentieth century a sorbet has come to mean a low-cal fruit ice, similar to a "sherbet," but with no dairy products added.

1/2 cup (3 1/2 oz.) granulated sugar
scant 1 cup (7 fl. oz.) water
1 tbsp. glucose syrup
18 oz. fresh blackcurrants

juice of 1 lemon
2 tbsp. crème de cassis
1 large egg white

Put sugar, water, and syrup in a pan, and heat gently until sugar dissolves, stirring occasionally. Simmer for 5 minutes, then set aside to cool.

Strip blackcurrants from their stalks and simmer in a pan with lemon juice until the currants "pop." Pour into a food processor or blender, add crème de cassis, and blend until smooth. Stir, pour into a freezer container, and freeze until firm around the edges. Transfer to a bowl and whisk to break up crystals. In another bowl, whisk egg white until standing in soft peaks, then whisk into blackcurrant mixture, 1 tablespoon at a time.

Return sorbet to freezer container, cover, and freeze again until solid. About 30 minutes before serving, transfer container to fridge to soften enough to be served in scoops.

Serves 8

red fruits slushy

see variations page 204

A food processor or blender with a powerful motor is needed to crush ice, so if you're unsure whether your machine is strong enough, break up the ice cubes first by placing them in a plastic bag and hitting them with a rolling pin or hammer. If you can't get fresh summer fruits, buy a package of mixed frozen berries and currants and blend them with the fruit juices while they are still solid, omitting the ice cubes.

18 oz. mixed summer fruits (e.g., strawberries, raspberries, black currants, red currants, blueberries, blackberries)
20 ice cubes

1/2 cup apple juice
1/2 cup orange juice
extra fruit, to serve

Prepare fruit as necessary by removing stalks and hulls. Put half the ice cubes in a food processor or blender, add fruit and fruit juices, and blend until ice is broken up. Add remaining ice cubes and blend again until mixture is slushy.

Spoon into glasses or serving dishes, top with extra fruit, and serve immediately before the ice has time to melt.

Serves 6

orange & cranberry ice pops

see variations page 205

These vividly colored ice pops not only look good, they taste good as well, and will appeal to both kids and grownups alike. As fruit juice freezes, it expands, so don't fill the molds quite to the top.

3 large oranges   **1 cup cranberry juice**

Peel oranges and divide into segments, removing all the pith and pips. In a food processor or blender, blend orange flesh until smooth. Pour into a measuring cup — you will need 1 cup to make the ice pops. If you don't have sufficient, top up by blending an extra orange or with orange juice.

Pour blended orange into 8 ice pop molds until they are half full. Freeze until juice is almost solid, but still just soft enough for the sticks to be pushed in and solid enough to hold the sticks in place.

Push in popsicle sticks and top off with cranberry juice. Do not fill all the way to the top. Return to freezer for several hours until frozen solid before carefully removing ice pops from molds.

Serves 8 (using 3-oz. molds)

variations

strawberry semifreddo

see base recipe page 173

apricot semifreddo
Prepare the basic recipe, replacing the strawberries with the same quantity of tinned apricot halves (drained weight). Purée the apricots in a food processor, rather than crushing them, the purée for the sauce doesn't need to be sieved.

strawberry & orange semifreddo
Prepare the basic recipe, whisking the finely grated zest of 1 orange with the cream and replacing the lemon juice with orange juice.

strawberry & liqueur semifreddo
Prepare the basic recipe, folding in 2 tablespoons brandy or orange liqueur with the cream.

strawberry & almond semifreddo
Prepare the basic recipe. Finely chop 3oz toasted almonds or hazelnuts and, with a palette knife, press them over the top and sides of the semifreddo.

fruits-of-the-forest semifreddo
Prepare the basic recipe, replacing 3/4 of the strawberries with a mix of other berries such as raspberries, blueberries, and blackcurrants. The mixed fruit can either be crushed with a potato masher or blended in a food processor.

variations

coconut malibu alaska

see base recipe page 174

raspberry & strawberry alaska
Prepare basic recipe, replacing the mango with 8 ounces raspberries, the coconut
liqueur with framboise liqueur, and vanilla ice cream with strawberry ice cream.

coconut, mango & chocolate alaska
Prepare basic recipe, replacing the vanilla ice cream with chocolate ice cream and
the gingerbread with plain chocolate cake.

rhubarb & orange alaska
Prepare basic recipe, replacing the mango with rhubarb. Chop 1 pound rhubarb
stalks into 1-inch lengths and cook in a pan with 3 ounces sugar and grated zest
and juice of 1 orange until soft. Cool completely before spooning into center of
the ice cream. Omit coconut liqueur.

toffee & peach alaska
Prepare basic recipe, replacing mango with 2 peeled, puréed peaches and
omitting coconut liqueur. Replace vanilla ice cream with toffee ice cream and
serve with toffee sauce.

coffee & apricot alaska
Prepare basic recipe, replacing mango with 5-6 puréed apricots and omitting
coconut liqueur. Use coffee ice cream instead of vanilla.

variations

blackberry & mint parfait with amaretti

see base recipe page 176

strawberry parfait with amaretti
Prepare basic recipe, replacing blackberries with strawberries and omitting mint. Serve with strawberry dessert sauce.

blueberry parfait with ginger crumbs
Prepare basic recipe, replacing blackberries with blueberries and replacing amaretti with crushed gingernaps. Serve with raspberry dessert sauce.

mango & lime parfait with amaretti
Prepare basic recipe, replacing blackberries with the same quantity of prepared mango flesh. Omit mint and use lime juice instead of lemon. Serve with strawberry dessert sauce. As mangoes are sweeter than blackberries, reduce the sugar by half or to taste.

peach & rosemary parfait with amaretti
Prepare basic recipe, replacing blackberries with chopped peaches. Replace mint with very finely chopped fresh rosemary. Serve with fresh orange slices.

fruits-of-the-forest parfait with amaretti
Prepare basic recipe, replacing blackberries with mixed berries and currants.

variations

brown bread & hazelnut ice cream

see base recipe page 178

brown bread & raisin ice cream
Prepare basic recipe, adding 3 ounces raisins with bread crumb mixture.

festive Christmas ice cream
Prepare basic recipe, adding 1 ounce each dried cranberries and golden raisins,
5 tablespoons chopped dried apricots, and 1 tablespoon finely chopped
crystallized orange peel with the bread crumb mixture.

brown bread, brandy & prune ice cream
Prepare basic recipe, soaking 6 ounces pitted, finely chopped prunes in
3 tablespoons brandy for 1 hour. Stir in prunes and their juice with the bread
crumb mixture.

atholl brose ice cream
Prepare basic recipe, replacing bread crumbs with rolled oats. Omit confectioners'
sugar and whip creams with 2 tablespoons whisky, instead of rum, and
4 tablespoons honey.

amaretti & hazelnut ice cream
Prepare basic recipe, omitting light brown sugar. Replace bread crumbs with
crushed amaretti, mixed with hazelnuts and cinnamon without baking in oven.
Replace rum with amaretto liqueur.

variations

espresso & almond praline semifreddo

see base recipe page 180

espresso & chocolate honeycomb semifreddo
Prepare basic recipe, replacing almond praline with 3 1/2 ounces chocolate
honeycomb candy such as Toblerone Honeycomb Crisp, chopped very finely.

espresso & hazelnut praline semifreddo
Prepare basic recipe, replacing almonds in praline with whole hazelnuts and
the amaretto with coffee liqueur. Serve with toasted chopped hazelnuts
instead of almonds.

espresso & chocolate chip semifreddo
Prepare basic recipe, omitting almond praline. Fold 3 1/2 ounces dark
chocolate chips in with whipped cream. Replace amaretto with brandy.

espresso, almond praline & orange semifreddo
Prepare basic recipe, replacing liqueur with orange juice. Whip grated zest of
1 orange with the cream.

espresso & amaretti semifreddo
Prepare basic recipe, replacing almond praline with 4 ounces crushed
amaretti and 3 ounces chopped toasted pecans. Scatter extra pecans over
finished dessert.

vanilla ice cream with black cherry compote

see base recipe page 183

vanilla & chocolate chip ice cream with black cherry compote
Prepare basic ice cream recipe, adding 3 1/2 ounces dark chocolate chips
when whisking partially frozen custard.

vanilla & lemon ripple ice cream with black cherry compote
Prepare basic ice cream recipe, whisking partially frozen custard and then
folding in 4 tablespoons lemon curd (page 109) before returning to freezer.

vanilla & peanut cookie ice cream with black cherry compote
Prepare basic recipe, whisking partially frozen custard then folding in
6 peanut butter cookies, crushed, before returning to freezer.

vanilla ice cream with strawberry compote
Prepare basic ice cream recipe, replacing cherry compote with strawberry
compote. Place 1 pound fresh strawberries in a bowl, sprinkle with 3
tablespoons confectioners' sugar and 2 tablespoons orange juice, and let
stand for 30 minutes before serving.

vanilla & prune ice cream with black cherry compote
Prepare basic recipe, freezing custard until partially frozen. Soak 6 pitted,
chopped prunes in 4 tablespoons green tea for 30 minutes. After whisking
semifrozen custard until smooth, fold in prunes and any tea remaining in
bowl before returning to freezer.

variations

limoncello ice cream

see base recipe page 184

orange liqueur ice cream
Prepare basic recipe, replacing lemons with 2 oranges. Replace limoncello with an orange liqueur such as Cointreau or Grand Marnier.

mojito ice cream
Prepare basic recipe, replacing lemons with 6 limes and 2 teaspoons chopped fresh mint. Replace limoncello with white rum.

harvey wallbanger ice cream
Prepare basic recipe, replacing lemons with 2 oranges and the limoncello with 1/4 cup vodka and 2 tablespoons Galliano.

piña colada ice cream
Prepare basic recipe, replacing lemons with 7 tablespoons pineapple juice and the limoncello with coconut liqueur.

margarita ice cream
Prepare basic recipe, replacing lemons with 6 limes and the limoncello with 4 tablespoons tequila and 4 tablespoons orange liqueur.

variations

peach melba yogurt ice

see base recipe page 185

pineapple raspberry yogurt ice
Prepare basic recipe, replacing peaches with roughly chopped flesh of
1 ripe pineapple.

mango raspberry yogurt ice
Prepare basic recipe, replacing peaches with flesh of 3 ripe mangoes, puréed
with juice of 2 limes rather than lemon juice.

nectarine blueberry yogurt ice
Prepare basic recipe, replacing peaches with nectarines and the raspberries
with blueberries.

apricot raspberry yogurt ice
Prepare basic recipe, replacing peaches with 12 apricots, halved and pitted.

apple blackberry yogurt ice
Prepare basic recipe, replacing peaches with roughly chopped apples, cooked
in a covered pan with lemon juice until soft enough to purée. Replace
raspberries with blackberries.

variations

pomegranate & lychee granita

see base recipe page 187

rhubarb granita
Prepare basic lychee granita recipe, replacing lychees with 1 pound rhubarb stalks cut into 1-inch lengths. Simmer rhubarb with water and sugar, increasing sugar by 6 ounces and adding grated zest of 1 orange. When soft, purée and freeze as for lychee granita. Omit pomegranate granita.

pink grapefruit granita
Prepare basic pomegranate granita recipe, replacing pomegranate juice with pink grapefruit juice and add 2 extra tablespoons sugar. Omit lychee granita.

apple-orange granita
Prepare basic recipe for pomegranate granita. Replace half the pomegranate juice with apple juice and half with orange juice. Omit lychee granita.

mango granita
Prepare basic recipe for lychee granita, replacing lychees with the same quantity of prepared mango flesh. Omit pomegranate granita.

papaya-lime granita
Prepare basic recipe for lychee granita, replacing lychees with the same quantity of prepared papaya flesh and adding grated zest and juice of 2 limes. Omit pomegranate granita.

variations

blackcurrant sorbet

see base recipe page 189

raspberry sorbet
Prepare basic recipe, replacing blackcurrants with raspberries and crème de cassis with framboise liqueur. Strain puréed raspberries to remove seeds.

chocolate sorbet
Prepare basic recipe, omitting blackcurrants, lemon juice, and crème de cassis. Increase the sugar to 6 ounces and the water to 2 cups. Put sugar, water, and syrup in a pan and whisk in 2 ounces cocoa powder. Bring to a boil and simmer for 5 minutes. Remove from heat and stir in 2 ounces chopped dark chocolate and 1 teaspoon vanilla extract until chocolate melts. Freeze and then whisk in the egg white.

lemon sorbet
Prepare basic recipe, omitting blackcurrants and crème de cassis. Increase sugar to 2 1/3 cups (1 pound) and water to 3 cups. Dissolve sugar in the water with the syrup and stir in 1 cup lemon juice and grated zest of 2 lemons. Simmer for 2–3 minutes. Cool, freeze, and whisk in egg white.

blueberry sorbet
Prepare basic recipe, replacing black currants with blueberries.

variations

red fruits slushy

see base recipe page 190

pear, apricot & banana slushy
Prepare basic recipe, replacing fruits with equal weight of chopped pears, apricots, and bananas. Replace apple juice with pineapple juice.

papaya, carrot & watermelon slushy
Prepare basic recipe, replacing fruits with equal weight of chopped papaya, watermelon, and bananas. Chop fruit into pieces and process with 2 tablespoons dried milk powder and equal quantities apple and carrot juice, and ice. Omit orange juice.

mango & pink grapefruit slushy
Prepare basic recipe, replacing fruits with 1 pound mango. Process with equal quantities orange and pink grapefruit juice and ice. Omit apple juice.

melon & lychee slushy
Prepare basic recipe, replacing fruits with 8 ounces cantaloupe melon and 8 ounces lychee flesh. Blend with 1 cup apple juice and ice. Omit orange juice.

nectarine & grape slushy
Prepare basic recipe, replacing fruits with equal weight of chopped nectarines and seedless green and red grapes and omitting juices. Blend with 1 cup white or red grape juice and ice.

variations

orange & cranberry ice pops

see base recipe page 193

pineapple & red grape ice pops
Prepare basic recipe, omitting oranges and cranberry juice. Use 1 cup
pineapple juice and 1 cup red grape juice.

cherry & kiwi ice pops
Prepare basic recipe, puréeing 4 ounces pitted black or dark red cherries
with 1 teaspoon honey and 4 ounces natural fromage frais to replace
orange juice. To replace cranberry juice, purée 4 ounces kiwi fruit flesh
with 1 teaspoon honey and 4 ounces natural fromage frais

banana, strawberry & coconut ice pops
Instead of basic recipe, purée 1 small, peeled and chopped banana with
6 ounces hulled strawberries, 3/4 cup milk, and 1/3 cup coconut milk. Pour
into molds and freeze.

mango & yogurt ice pops
Instead of the basic recipe, purée the flesh of 1 ripe mango with 1/2 cup
light cream and 5 ounces natural yogurt. Pour into molds and freeze.

pomegranate & grapefruit ice pops
Instead of basic recipe, use 1 cup pomegranate juice and 1 cup
grapefruit juice.

cookies, brownies, shortcakes & whoopie pies

Small enough to satisfy young appetites, grown-up enough for adults to savor — no one will be able to resist caramel and pecan turtle brownies, vanilla whoopie pies, peanut butter cookie and ice cream sandwiches, and all the other treats on the following pages.

rocky road cookies

see variations page 223

These will be a guaranteed hit with children and adults alike. They can be served on their own or with scoops of your favorite ice cream.

4 oz. dark chocolate, chopped
1 tbsp. light corn syrup
1/2 cup (4 oz.) unsalted butter, cut into small
    pieces
2 oz. cream cheese
12 graham crackers, in small pieces

1/2 cup (3 oz.) dried apricots, chopped
3 tbsp. (1 oz.) dried cranberries
1/2 cup (2 oz.) chopped pecans
2 1/3 cups (4 oz.) mini marshmallows
2 oz. milk chocolate, melted

Put dark chocolate, corn syrup, and butter in a large saucepan (one that will be big enough to hold all the ingredients). Heat gently until melted, stirring from time to time until smooth. Remove from heat and stir in cream cheese until evenly combined. Add broken cookies, dried apricots, cranberries, pecans, and about three-quarters of the marshmallows. Stir well until all ingredients are well coated.

Line cups of a 12-cup muffin pan with plastic wrap. Spoon in mixture, pressing it down with the back of the spoon. Top with remaining marshmallows and let set in the fridge.

Lift cookies carefully out of the cups and peel off plastic wrap. Drizzle melted milk chocolate over the top of cookies. Let set again.

Makes 12

lemon & poppy seed shortbread fingers with plums & cherries

see variations page 224

The secret of good shortbread is to work in a cool kitchen and handle the dough as lightly as you possibly can. Too much kneading or processing, and the end result will be heavy and solid rather than buttery, melt-in-the-mouth, and crisp.

for the shortbread
3/4 cup (6 oz.) unsalted butter, softened
7 tbsp. (3 oz.) granulated sugar,
    plus extra to dust
finely grated zest of 1 lemon
2 tbsp. poppy seeds
1 3/4 cups (6 oz.) all-purpose flour
1/2 cup (3 oz.) rice flour

for the fruit
8 red plums, halved and pitted
8 oz. red cherries, pitted
scant 1 cup (7 oz.) apple juice
1 red fruit tea bag (e.g., raspberry,
    cherry, strawberry)

Preheat oven to 300°F. Grease a shallow 7x11-inch pan and line base with parchment. To make the shortbread, beat butter, sugar, and lemon zest together until light and creamy. Add poppy seeds, sift in the flours, and work mixture together lightly by hand (or in a food processor). Transfer to pan, and with floured hands, press mixture to fill pan evenly. Prick surface all over with a fork and bake for 45 minutes until pale golden brown. Dust top with sugar and mark cut lines for squares or triangles. Cool in pan for 15 minutes before lifting shortbread onto a wire rack to cool completely. Remove lining paper and cut into pieces. To cook the plums and cherries, put fruit in a pan, pour in apple juice, and tuck tea bag under plum halves to keep it from floating. Bring to a boil, then remove from heat. Cover pan and let fruit cool in the liquid. Remove tea bag and serve fruit with shortbread.
Makes 6

caramel & pecan turtle brownies

see variations page 225

If you think brownies are just an everyday treat to nibble with coffee, this "millionaire" version is set to change your mind. Decadently rich and dark with a golden toffee and nut topping, these brownies are the ultimate feel-good dessert.

for the brownies
3 1/2 oz. dark chocolate, chopped
3/4 cup (6 oz.) unsalted butter, cut up
3 large eggs, beaten
3/4 cup (5 1/2 oz.) dark brown sugar
1/2 cup (2 oz.) flour
1 tsp. baking powder
1/2 cup (2 oz.) roughly chopped pecans
4 tbsp. (2 oz.) white chocolate chips

for the topping
scant 1 cup (6 oz.) granulated sugar
2 tbsp. cold water
3/4 cup (6 fl. oz.) heavy cream
1 tsp. vanilla extract
10 tbsp. (5 oz.) unsalted butter
1 cup (4 oz.) roughly chopped pecans
4 oz. dark or milk chocolate chunks

Preheat oven to 350°F. Grease an 8-inch loose-bottomed square cake pan and line the base and sides with parchment. Melt dark chocolate and butter in a pan over a gentle heat until melted, stirring occasionally until smooth. Let cool for 10 minutes. Beat in eggs, brown sugar, flour, baking powder, pecans, and white chocolate chips until evenly combined. Pour into pan and bake for 30 minutes until crusty on top but still soft underneath. Let cool in pan. To make the topping, heat sugar and water, bring to a boil and bubble until syrup caramelizes to a dark brown. Remove from heat and gradually beat in cream. (If caramel sets in hard lumps, microwave mixture on medium power to re-melt, stirring every 30 seconds.) Add vanilla. In a separate bowl, beat butter until creamy. Gradually beat in caramel mixture. Let cool completely and then chill until spreadable. Spread topping over brownies, scatter pecans and chocolate chunks on top, and let set before removing from pan and cutting into squares.
Makes 9

chocolate brownie gâteau

see variations page 226

The perfect dessert that can also double as a birthday cake for anyone who finds chocolate brownies irresistible — and, let's face it, that means most of us! Keep an eye on the brownie layers towards the end of the cooking time. If they're left too long in the oven, the centers will dry out rather than remaining gooey and dark.

1 cup plus 2 tbsp. (9 oz.) unsalted butter,
   softened
9 oz. dark chocolate, chopped
4 large eggs
1 1/4 cups (9 oz.) light brown sugar
1/2 tsp. vanilla extract

1 3/4 cups (6 oz.) flour
1 cup plus 3 tbsp. (7 oz.) whole hazelnuts,
   chopped
for the filling
1/2 cup crème fraîche
3 1/2 oz. white chocolate, chopped

Preheat oven to 350°F. Grease, then line bases of two 8-inch cake pans with baking parchment. In a saucepan, heat butter and chocolate gently until melted, stirring until smooth. Set aside to cool for 10 minutes. Beat together eggs, sugar, and vanilla, and add to chocolate mixture with flour and hazelnuts. Stir until evenly combined. Divide mixture between cake pans. Bake for 25–30 minutes or until the tops have a pale crust but the middle is still quite soft. Place a sheet of waxed paper on a cooling rack. Loosen edges of brownie layers with a knife and turn upside down onto rack, still in the pans. Let cool before removing pans and lining paper. To make the filling, heat crème fraîche and white chocolate gently until chocolate melts. Stir until smooth, transfer to a bowl, and let cool and thicken until it holds its shape. Whisk cooled filling until light and creamy, and use to sandwich brownie layers together.

Serves 12

vanilla whoopie pies

see variations page 227

These cookie-like cakes filled with marshmallow frosting are an all-American favorite adored by kids and adults alike. Perfect for lunch boxes and parties alike.

1 large egg
3/4 cup (5 1/2 oz.) granulated sugar
6 tbsp. (3 oz.) unsalted butter, melted
    and cooled
2 3/4 cups (10 oz.) flour
3/4 tsp. baking soda
scant 1 cup (7 oz.) buttermilk
1 tsp. vanilla extract

for the filling
2 large egg whites
heaping 1/2 cup (4 oz.) granulated sugar
1/2 tsp. cream of tartar
2 1/4 cups (4 oz.) white or pink marshmallows
for the topping
1 1/3 cups (6 oz.) confectioners' sugar
about 2 tbsp. lemon juice
sugar sprinkles

Preheat oven to 350°F. Line 2 baking sheets with parchment. In a mixing bowl, whisk egg and sugar until pale and creamy. Drizzle melted butter around edge of mixture and fold in. Sift in half the flour with the baking soda and fold in with half the buttermilk. Sift in remaining flour, add remaining buttermilk, and the vanilla, and fold in all ingredients. Drop 24 small spoonfuls of the mixture well spaced on the baking sheets, and bake for about 15 minutes until springy. Cool for 10 minutes before removing from baking sheet to a wire rack. To make the filling, whisk egg whites, sugar, and cream of tartar together in a bowl set over a pan of simmering water for about 5 minutes until thickened. Add marshmallows and stir to melt, then whisk for another 2 minutes until shiny and smooth. Let cool. Use to sandwich whoopie pies together in pairs. To make the topping, sift confectioners' sugar into a bowl and stir in enough lemon juice to make a spreadable frosting. Spread a little over the top of each whoopie pie and scatter on sugar sprinkles. Store in an airtight container.
Makes 12

giant chocolate & orange whoopie pie

see variations page 228

For this party-size pie, a white chocolate filling replaces traditional marshmallow.

2 3/4 cups (10 oz.) flour
1/2 cup (2 oz.) unsweetened cocoa powder
1 tsp. baking powder
1/2 tsp. baking soda
1/2 cup (4 oz.) unsalted butter
7 tbsp. (3 oz.) dark brown sugar
3/4 cup (5 oz.) granulated sugar
finely grated zest of 1 orange
2 large eggs
1/2 cup sour cream
2 tbsp. milk

for the filling
4 oz. full-fat cream cheese
4 tbsp. (1 1/2 oz.) granulated sugar
3 1/2 oz. white chocolate, melted
6 tbsp. heavy cream, whipped
for the frosting
1 3/4 cups (8 oz.) confectioners' sugar, sifted
about 3 tbsp. orange juice
few drops of orange food coloring
grated chocolate or chocolate curls

Preheat oven to 350°F. Draw two 7-inch circles on two sheets of baking parchment and place on baking sheets. Sift together flour, cocoa powder, baking powder, and baking soda. In a bowl, beat butter, sugars, and orange zest together until creamy. Gradually beat in eggs, then stir in dry ingredients alternating with sour cream and milk. Spoon mixture onto baking sheets and spread to fill circles. Bake for 20 minutes until firm. Cool for 10 minutes before transferring to wire rack. To make filling, beat cream cheese and sugar until smooth. Add melted chocolate and fold in with cream. Use to sandwich cake layers together. To make frosting, mix confectioners' sugar with enough orange juice to make smooth frosting. Tint with orange food coloring and spoon over cake. Scatter with grated chocolate or curls.
Serves 10

strawberries & cream shortcakes

see variations page 229

Make sure you leave plenty of room at the end of the meal for one – or more – of these indulgent treats, as they're impossible to resist. Make the shortcakes ahead and assemble with the cream and strawberries about 30 minutes before serving.

for the shortcakes
1/2 cup (4 oz.) unsalted butter, cut into
    small pieces
3 1/3 cups (13 oz.) self-rising flour
1/2 cup (4 oz.) granulated sugar
1/3 cup warm milk, plus a little extra milk
    for glazing

1 large egg, beaten
1/2 tsp. vanilla extract
1 tbsp. lemon juice
for the filling
1 generous cup whipping or heavy cream
3 tbsp. strawberry jam
10 oz. fresh strawberries

Put butter and flour in mixing bowl and rub together until consistency of bread crumbs. Stir in sugar, warm milk, beaten egg, vanilla, and lemon juice. Mix to make a soft, smooth dough. Preheat oven to 425°F. On a lightly floured surface, roll out dough about 3/4 inch thick. Cut out 8 rounds using a 2 1/2-inch plain or fluted pastry cutter, gathering up trimmings of dough and rerolling as needed. Lift dough rounds onto a greased baking sheet and brush tops with milk to glaze. Bake for 10-12 minutes or until well risen and golden brown. The shortcakes are cooked when they sound hollow if tapped on the base. Transfer to a wire rack to cool. Whip cream until it holds its shape. Split each shortcake in half and spread the bottom halves with jam. Spoon on cream, then add sliced strawberries and top halves of the shortcakes.

Makes 8

peanut butter cookie & ice cream sandwiches

see variations page 230

The cookies can be made several days ahead and stored in an airtight container. Any ice cream can be used to sandwich the cookies together, so just pick your family's favorite.

for the cookies
9 tbsp. (4 1/2 oz.) unsalted butter, softened
1/2 tsp vanilla extract
finely grated zest of 1/2 lemon
7 tbsp. (3 oz.) granulated sugar
2 tbsp. (1 oz.) light brown sugar
1/2 cup (3 oz.) crunchy peanut butter
1 3/4 cups (6 oz.) flour
1 tsp. baking soda

2 tbsp. (1 oz.) unsalted peanuts, chopped
for the filling
1 tub of ice cream of your choice, softened
for the chocolate sauce
4 oz. dark chocolate, chopped
1 tbsp. unsalted butter, cut up
3 tbsp. milk

To make cookies, preheat the oven to 350°F. Grease 2 or 3 baking sheets and line with parchment. Cream together butter, vanilla, lemon zest, sugar, brown sugar, and peanut butter. Sift in flour and baking soda and stir in peanuts, working with your hands to make a soft dough. With floured hands, roll dough into 20 small balls and place on baking sheets, well spaced apart. Press down lightly on top of each with a fork. Bake for 15–20 minutes until light golden. Let cool on baking sheets. For filling, sandwich cookies together in pairs with a scoop of ice cream, pressing the top cookie down gently. Place in freezer and freeze until ice cream is firm. To make the chocolate sauce, gently heat chocolate, butter, and milk in a pan until chocolate and butter melt, stirring regularly until smooth. When ready to serve, place ice cream sandwiches on serving plates and drizzle with chocolate sauce.
Makes 10

fruit & nut chocolate slices with crème fraîche

see variations page 231

Macadamia nuts with their buttery, almost shortbread-like flavor, turn these simple chocolate slices, which are somewhere between a mousse and a cake, into something special. If you like the current craze for adding salted nuts or salt caramel to chocolate bars, try using salted macadamias, but if not, the plain variety are readily available.

7 oz. dark chocolate, chopped
3/4 cup (5 1/2 oz.) dark brown sugar
3/4 cup (6 oz.) unsalted butter, cut up
1/2 cup milk
1 tsp. vanilla extract
3 large eggs, beaten

1/2 cup (3 oz.) raisins
1/2 cup (3 oz.) macadamia nuts,
    roughly chopped
crème fraîche, grated chocolate,
    and confectioners' sugar, to serve

Preheat oven to 350°F. Grease an 8-inch square pan and line base and sides with nonstick baking parchment. Place chocolate in a pan with brown sugar, butter, and milk. Heat gently until melted, stirring occasionally until smooth. Remove from heat and let cool for 10 minutes. Beat in vanilla extract and eggs until evenly mixed, and then stir in raisins and chopped macadamia nuts. Pour mixture into prepared pan and bake for 30–35 minutes or until the top is firm when lightly pressed. Let cool in the pan, then transfer to the fridge and chill for 3–4 hours or longer. Remove cake from pan and peel off lining paper. Cut into 8 large or 12 smaller fingers and serve with crème fraîche with grated chocolate sprinkled over the top, and a light dusting of confectioners' sugar.

Serves 8–12

variations

rocky road cookies

see base recipe page 207

rocky road milk chocolate cookies
Prepare basic recipe, replacing the dark chocolate with milk chocolate and drizzling with white chocolate instead of milk chocolate.

rocky road cookies with crunchy seeds
Prepare basic recipe, adding a mixture of seeds such as sunflower, sesame, and pumpkin in place of the dried apricots and cranberries.

rocky road meringue cookies
Prepare basic recipe, replacing marshmallows with 8 small crushed meringues and stirring them into the mixture.

rocky road ginger cookies
Prepare basic recipe, replacing graham crackers with gingersnaps.

rocky road cinnamon cookies
Prepare basic recipe, adding 1 teaspoon ground cinnamon to the dark chocolate, syrup, and butter mixture.

lemon & poppy seed shortbread fingers with plums & cherries

see base recipe page 208

orange & poppy seed shortbread fingers with plums & cherries
Prepare basic shortbread recipe, replacing lemon zest with orange zest.

lemon & sesame seed shortbread fingers with plums & cherries
Prepare basic shortbread recipe, replacing poppy seeds with sesame seeds.

lemon, poppy seed & almond shortbread fingers with plums & cherries
Prepare basic shortbread recipe, replacing rice flour with ground almonds.

lemon, poppy seed & chocolate shortbread fingers with plums & cherries
Prepare basic shortbread recipe, drizzling baked, cooled shortbread fingers with 3 ounces melted dark chocolate.

lemon & hazelnut wholemeal shortbread fingers with plums & cherries
Prepare basic shortbread recipe, replacing half the all-purpose flour with whole wheat flour and the poppy seeds with ground hazelnuts.

variations

caramel & pecan turtle brownies

see base recipe page 210

cardamom-spiced turtle brownies
Prepare basic recipe, adding 1 teaspoon ground cardamom to dark chocolate and butter mixture.

caramel & walnut turtle brownies
Prepare basic recipe, replacing pecans with walnuts.

pecan brownies with chocolate fudge frosting
Prepare basic recipe, replacing caramel topping with chocolate fudge frosting. Heat 2 ounces sweet butter with 3 tablespoons milk and 1 ounce cocoa powder until melted. Sift in 7 ounces confectioners' sugar, beating well after each addition. Let frosting cool and thicken, then beat before spreading over brownies.

caramel, pecan & golden raisin turtle brownies
Prepare basic recipe, using golden raisins instead of white chocolate chips.

vanilla-iced pecan brownies
Prepare basic recipe, replacing caramel topping on brownies with vanilla-flavored glacé icing. Sift 7 ounces confectioners' sugar into a bowl and stir in 1/2 teaspoon vanilla extract and enough cold water to make a smooth icing that can be drizzled over brownies.

variations

chocolate brownie gâteau

see base recipe page 212

chocolate pecan brownie gâteau
Prepare basic recipe, replacing chopped hazelnuts with chopped pecans.

chocolate brownie gâteau with dark chocolate cream
Prepare basic recipe, replacing white chocolate in the filling with
dark chocolate.

chocolate brownie gâteau with raspberries and white chocolate cream
Prepare basic recipe, spreading bottom brownie layer with half the filling
and then scattering over 4 ounces fresh raspberries. Add remaining filling
and top with second brownie layer.

chocolate raisin brownie gâteau
Prepare basic recipe, replacing chopped hazelnuts with raisins.

chocolate orange brownie gâteau
Prepare basic recipe, adding finely grated zest of 1 orange to brownie batter
and serving the gâteau with fresh orange segments.

variations

vanilla whoopie pies

see base recipe page 215

vanilla whoopie pies with lemon buttercream
Prepare basic recipe, filling whoopie pies with lemon buttercream instead of marshmallow cream. Beat 4 ounces sweet butter until softened. Gradually beat in 8 ounces sifted confectioners' sugar until smooth, adding the juice of 1/2 lemon to make a soft spreadable icing.

red, white & blue velvet whoopie pies
Prepare basic recipe, adding 1 tablespoon blue food coloring to the batter and coloring the topping red.

almond whoopie pies
Prepare basic recipe, replacing vanilla extract in batter with almond extract. Scatter chopped toasted almonds over the pies rather than sugar sprinkles.

vanilla whoopie pies with cream cheese filling
Prepare basic recipe, replacing marshmallow filling with cream cheese filling. Beat together 4 ounces full-fat cream cheese, 2 ounces sweet butter, and 8 ounces sifted confectioners' sugar.

chocolate whoopie pies
Prepare basic recipe, replacing 2 tablespoons of flour in the batter with cocoa.

variations

giant chocolate & orange whoopie pie

see base recipe page 216

giant ginger & orange whoopie pie
Prepare basic recipe, omitting cocoa powder, increasing flour to 12 ounces, and add 1 teaspoon ground ginger with the other dry ingredients.

giant chocolate & hazelnut whoopie pie
Prepare basic recipe, replacing 2 ounces flour with ground hazelnuts.

giant chocolate & orange whoopie pie with dark chocolate filling
Prepare basic recipe, substituting melted dark chocolate for the white chocolate in the filling.

giant chocolate & raspberry whoopie pie
Prepare basic recipe, folding 4 ounces lightly crushed raspberries into filling with the whipped cream. For the icing, replace orange juice and orange food coloring with cranberry juice or grenadine syrup.

giant lemon, mint & chocolate whoopie pie
Prepare basic recipe, replacing orange zest in batter with grated zest of 2 lemons. Replace orange juice in icing with lemon juice and the orange food coloring with a few drops of peppermint flavoring.

variations

strawberries & cream shortcakes

see base recipe page 219

melba cream shortcakes
Prepare basic recipe, replacing strawberry jelly with seedless raspberry jelly and strawberries with 1 peeled and sliced peach and 5 ounces raspberries.

strawberries & cream orange shortcakes
Prepare basic recipe, replacing lemon juice in shortcake dough with orange juice and whipping the finely grated zest of 1 orange into cream for filling.

golden raisin shortcakes with cherries & cream
Prepare basic recipe. Add 2 ounces golden raisins to dough. Replace strawberries with pitted cherries and strawberry jelly with cherry jelly.

nutty shortcakes with strawberries & cream
Prepare basic recipe, scattering chopped almonds, pine nuts, or pecans over tops of shortcakes after glazing with milk.

cinnamon shortcakes with strawberries & cream
Prepare basic recipe, adding 1 teaspoon ground cinnamon to shortcake dough with the flour.

variations

peanut butter cookie & ice cream sandwiches

see base recipe page 220

cashew butter cookie & ice cream sandwiches
Prepare basic recipe, replacing peanuts with chopped unsalted cashews and the peanut butter with cashew butter.

peanut butter cookie & ice cream sandwiches with strawberry sauce
Prepare basic recipe, filling the sandwiches with strawberry ice cream and drizzling with strawberry sauce made by puréeing 4 ounces fresh strawberries with 1 tablespoon confectioners' sugar.

chocolate chip cookie & ice cream sandwiches
Prepare basic recipe, replacing peanuts with 5 tablespoons milk chocolate chips and the crunchy peanut butter with smooth.

peanut butter raisin cookie & ice cream sandwiches
Prepare basic recipe, replacing peanuts with 2 ounces raisins.

orange peanut cookie and ice cream sandwiches
Prepare basic recipe, replacing lemon zest and vanilla extract in cookie dough with finely grated zest of 1/2 orange.

variations

fruit & nut chocolate slices with crème fraîche

see base recipe page 222

chocolate apricot slices with crème fraîche
Prepare basic recipe, replacing macadamia nuts with chopped dried apricots.

milk chocolate fruit & nut slices with crème fraîche
Prepare basic recipe, replacing dark chocolate with good-quality milk chocolate, the raisins with dried cranberries, and the macadamias with chopped unsalted peanuts.

double chocolate & nut slices with crème fraîche
Prepare basic recipe, replacing raisins with 1/2 cup (3 ounces) white chocolate chips.

chocolate almond slices with crème fraîche
Prepare basic recipe, replacing raisins and macadamia nuts with 1/2 cup chopped or slivered almonds and 1/2 cup finely chopped crystallized citrus peel or glacé cherries.

fruit & nut chocolate slices with orange crème fraîche
Prepare basic recipe, stirring the finely grated zest of 1 small orange into the crème fraîche.

fritters, crêpes & waffles

Crisp and light fritters, melt-in-the-mouth crêpes

and waffles to die for — this chapter will satisfy all

your comfort food cravings.

fruit tempura

see variations page 248

Unlike most batters, light tempura batter needs to be used as soon as it is made rather than left to stand. It's also important to use chilled water straight from the fridge – sparkling mineral water works best – and not to fry too many pieces of fruit at one time or the temperature of the oil will drop and the batter will be soggy rather than crisp.

2 lbs. fresh, ripe, but firm fruit such as peaches, apricots, bananas, plums, cherries, pineapple
for the orange cream
scant 1 cup (7 fl. oz.) heavy cream
finely grated zest and juice of 1 orange
for the batter
scant 1 cup (3 oz.) flour, plus extra for dusting

1 tbsp. cornstarch
1 tsp. baking powder
2 tsp. sugar
scant 1 cup (7 fl. oz.) well-chilled sparkling mineral water
vegetable or peanut oil for deep-frying

Prepare the fruit by peeling and pitting as necessary. Cut into two-bite-size slices, wedges or chunks, or leave whole if small. To make the orange cream, whip cream, half the orange zest, and the juice together until holding its shape. Spoon into a serving dish, sprinkle with remaining zest, and chill, covered with plastic wrap, until needed. To make the batter, sift flour, cornstarch, and baking powder into a bowl. Stir in sugar. Whisk in water until just combined. Don't overmix the batter – it doesn't matter if it is still a little bit lumpy. Heat oil for deep-frying to 375°F. Dust fruit with flour, dip in batter, and fry 3–4 pieces at a time for 2–3 minutes or until pale golden and crisp. Drain on a plate lined with absorbent paper towels. Serve immediately with orange cream.

Serves 4

blueberry fritters with apricot sauce

see variations page 249

When fresh apricots are unavailable, the sauce can be made with canned fruit. Simply blend the contents of 1 (14-oz.) can of apricot halves in fruit juice (fruit and juice) with 1 tablespoon honey until smooth and then warm in a saucepan when needed.

for the sauce
11 oz. fresh apricots, halved and pitted
scant 1 cup (7 fl. oz.) apple juice
1 tbsp. honey
for the fritters
5 1/2 oz. fresh blueberries

4 oz. fresh raspberries
scant 1 cup (3 oz.) flour
2 tbsp. milk
1 large egg
2 tbsp. sugar, plus extra to dust
vegetable or peanut oil for deep-frying

To make the sauce, simmer apricot halves in a pan with apple juice and honey for about 10 minutes until softened. Pour into blender and blend until smooth. Return to the pan and set aside while you make fritters. To make the fritters, in a bowl, mix together blueberries, raspberries, and flour. In another bowl, whisk together milk, egg, and sugar, and stir into fruit mixture to make a thick batter. Mix well so all the ingredients are combined. Meanwhile, heat oil for deep-frying to 350°F. Drop spoonfuls of batter into hot oil and fry for 1–2 minutes, turning over once or twice until golden. Drain on a plate lined with paper towels and keep warm in a low oven while you continue frying, to make 12 fritters. Reheat sauce over low heat. Divide warm fritters between 4 serving plates and spoon the sauce alongside. Dust with sugar and serve immediately.

Serves 4

chinese toffee pineapple & bananas

see variations page 250

A classic Chinese dessert that is a mainstay of Cantonese restaurant menus. The soft sweet fruit encased in crunchy caramel and sesame seeds is a real delight.

heaping 1/2 cup (4 oz.) flour, plus extra
    for dusting
about 1/2 cup cold water
2 tsp. vegetable or peanut oil, plus extra for
    deep-frying
3 pineapple rings, canned or fresh

2 large, ripe but firm, bananas
sesame oil for greasing
ice cubes
1 3/4 cups (12 oz.) sugar
3/4 cup (6 fl. oz.) water
3 tbsp. sesame seeds

Sift flour into a bowl and whisk in enough cold water to make a smooth batter. Stir in oil. Let stand for 30 minutes. Cut each pineapple ring into quarters. Peel bananas and cut each into 6 equal chunks. Heat oil for deep-frying to 375°F. Dust fruit with flour and drop about 6 pieces into the batter. Lift them out one at a time with a slotted spoon and carefully lower into hot oil. Adding the fruit pieces one at a time keeps them from sticking together as they fry. Fry fruit for 2–3 minutes until golden, then remove with a slotted spoon and drain on a plate lined with paper towels. Repeat with remaining fruit. Grease a large plate with a little sesame oil and have ready a bowl filled with cold water and ice cubes. To make toffee coating, gently heat sugar in a heavy pan with the water, until melted, bring to a boil and boil until syrup caramelizes to golden brown. Remove pan from heat and add sesame seeds and fruit pieces, turning them over until they are well coated. Immediately turn out onto the greased plate, and use 2 forks to dip fruit into the iced water to set toffee coating. Serve immediately.
Serves 4

thai coconut balls with watermelon, star fruit & pomegranate seeds

see variations page 251

As the fried coconut balls cool, they will absorb the hot syrup and become temptingly sweet and sticky. They are best eaten still slightly warm rather than chilled.

for the coconut balls
heaping 1/2 cup (4 oz.) flour
1/2 tsp. baking powder
6 tbsp. coconut milk powder
4 tbsp. (2 oz.) unsalted butter, cut into
    small pieces
about 4 tbsp. coconut milk or cow's milk
vegetable or peanut oil for deep-frying

for the syrup
generous 1 cup (8 oz.) sugar
4 tbsp. water
1 tsp. coconut flavoring
to serve:
1 slice watermelon
2 pineapple rings
seeds from 1 pomegranate
2 tbsp. grated fresh coconut

To make the coconut balls, sift flour, baking powder, and coconut milk powder into a bowl. Rub in butter until consistency of bread crumbs, then add enough milk to mix to a smooth, soft dough. Divide dough into 16 equal pieces and roll into balls.

Heat oil for deep-frying to 350°F. Fry coconut balls in batches for about 5 minutes or until they are golden brown. Remove with a slotted spoon and let drain on a plate lined with paper towels, then transfer to a large heatproof bowl.

To make the syrup, gently heat sugar and water in a pan until sugar dissolves. Bring to a boil and simmer for 1 minute. Stir in coconut flavoring. Pour hot syrup over coconut balls. Set aside to cool.

To serve, chop watermelon into chunks. Chop pineapple rings. Divide coconut balls between serving plates and drizzle with any syrup remaining in bowl. Serve coconut balls with watermelon and pineapple, and scatter pomegranate seeds and grated coconut on top.

Serves 4

cinnamon beignets with blueberry sauce

see variations page 252

These crisp, golden puffs simply melt in your mouth and are deliciously addictive. Like most fritters, they are best eaten immediately.

for the sauce
1 lb. fresh blackberries
1/2 cup plus 2 tbsp. cold water
4 tbsp. (2 oz.) sugar
juice of 1 orange
1 tbsp. arrowroot
for the beignets
heaping 1/2 cup (4 oz.) flour

1 tsp. ground cinnamon
1/2 cup water
4 tbsp. (2 oz.) unsalted butter, cut into pieces
2 medium eggs, beaten
finely grated zest of 1/2 orange
1 tbsp. sugar
vegetable or peanut oil for deep-frying
confectioners' sugar, to dust

To make sauce, heat blackberries in a pan with 1/2 cup water, sugar, and orange juice. Cover and simmer for 10 minutes and set aside. Mix arrowroot with 2 tablespoons cold water and set aside. To make beignets, sift flour and cinnamon onto a plate. Heat water and butter in a pan until melted. Bring to a fast boil, remove from heat, and tip in all the flour. Beat vigorously with a wooden spoon until mixture forms a smooth ball. Cool for a few minutes, then gradually beat in eggs. Beat in orange zest and sugar. Heat oil for deep-frying to 325°F. Drop teaspoonfuls of batter into hot oil and fry beignets in batches for 4–5 minutes until puffed and golden. Remove with a slotted spoon and drain on plate lined with paper towels. Stir arrowroot mixture until smooth and mix into sauce. Reheat sauce over low heat until thickened. Serve beignets warm with sauce and dusted with confectioners' sugar.
Serves 4

orange crêpes with pears & grapes

see variations page 253

The pears should be ripe but still firm, as if they're too soft they'll turn mushy and start to fall apart in the sauce. Any variety of pear can be used.

for the crêpes
heaping 1/2 cup (4 oz.) flour
1 tbsp. sugar
finely grated zest of 1 orange
2 large eggs
scant 1 cup (7 fl. oz.) milk
6 tbsp. water
2 tbsp. unsalted butter, melted, plus extra
   butter for frying

for the sauce
2 oranges
7 tbsp. (3 oz.) sugar
juice of 1 lemon
4 tbsp. (2 oz.) unsalted butter, cut up
2 pears, peeled, cored, and sliced
4 oz. seedless grapes

To make crêpes, sift flour into a bowl and stir in sugar and orange zest. Make a well in center of the flour, add eggs, and whisk. Mix milk and water and whisk into the crêpe mixture. Stir in 2 tablespoons melted butter, pour into pitcher, and set aside for 30 minutes. To cook crêpes, melt a little butter in a 7 or 8-inch nonstick skillet and pour in a little batter, swirling to coat the base. Cook for 1–2 minutes until underside is golden, and flip over to cook other side. Slide crêpe off pan onto a plate and keep warm. Cook rest of batter to make 12 crêpes. To make sauce, slice zest from 1 orange into fine strips. Set aside. Squeeze juice from both oranges and add to a pan with sugar and lemon juice. Cook until sugar dissolves, then add butter. Add pear and grapes with zest, and baste with juices. Cook for 1–2 minutes until pears soften. Serve crêpes with hot fruit and juices spooned over.
Serves 6

choc 'n' nut crêpes

see variations page 254

The chocolate sauce on these crêpes makes them richer and perfect for a special treat. As with the previous crêpe recipe, these are best eaten as soon as possible after cooking.

for the crêpes
heaping 1/2 cup (4 oz.) flour
2 large eggs
scant 1 cup (7 fl. oz.) milk
6 tbsp. cold water
1 tbsp. sugar
2 tbsp. unsalted butter, melted, plus extra
    butter for frying

for the chocolate sauce
5 1/2 oz. milk or dark chocolate, chopped
1 1/4 cups (5 1/2 oz.) plain yogurt
1/2 tsp. vanilla extract
to serve
toasted pine nuts
fresh raspberries

To make crêpes, sift flour into a mixing bowl, make a well in the center, and add eggs. Whisk until eggs start to combine with flour. Mix the milk and water together and gradually whisk in. Add sugar and melted butter and whisk until smooth. Transfer batter to pitcher and set aside for 30 minutes. To make chocolate sauce, melt chocolate in a bowl over a pan of hot water until smooth. Remove bowl from heat and whisk in yogurt and vanilla. Set aside. To cook crêpes, grease a 7 or 8-inch nonstick skillet with butter and pour in a little batter, swirling pan so it coats the base in a thin layer. Cook for 1–2 minutes until underside is golden, and flip over to cook other side. Slide crêpe off pan onto a plate and keep them warm. Cook remaining mixture to make 12-16 crêpes. Fold or roll crêpes and divide between serving plates. Drizzle with chocolate sauce and scatter with a generous amount of toasted pine nuts and fresh raspberries.

Serves 4

chocolate chip waffles

see variations page 255

The smell of these cooking will get everyone out of bed in double-quick time.

for the chocolate sauce
1 1/4 cups heavy cream
8 oz. bittersweet chocolate, broken into pieces
1 tbsp. light corn syrup
for the waffles
1 1/2 cups flour
1 1/2 tsp. baking powder

2 tbsp. sugar
1/2 cup semisweet chocolate chips
1/2 tsp. salt
1 1/4 cups milk
2 large eggs
5 tbsp. butter, melted, plus extra for cooking
powdered sugar, to serve

To make the chocolate sauce, heat the cream in a medium saucepan until almost boiling. Add the chocolate and corn syrup, and stir until the chocolate has melted and the sauce is smooth and creamy. Serve hot or cold.

Preheat the waffle iron. In a large bowl, using a fork, mix together the flour, baking powder, sugar, chocolate chips, and salt. In another bowl, whisk the milk and eggs together, then pour into the flour mixture. Mix together with the fork until there are no large lumps, but do not overmix. Stir in the 5 tablespoons melted butter. When the iron is hot, lightly brush it with some melted butter, then spoon in enough batter to just cover the base. Remember the batter will rise and spread during cooking. Cook for 3-5 minutes, until crisp. Keep warm while you make the rest. Serve immediately, sprinkled with a little powdered sugar and with the chocolate sauce on the side.

Makes 8 waffles

variations

fruit tempura

see base recipe page 233

fruit tempura with green tea cream
Prepare basic recipe, replacing orange zest and juice with 2 tablespoons confectioners' sugar and 1 teaspoon powdered green tea.

fruit tempura with raspberry sauce
Prepare basic recipe, serving tempura with raspberry sauce instead of orange cream. Simmer 1 pound raspberries with 4 ounces sugar until soft, then push through a sieve and discard seeds.

hazelnut-filled plum & apricot tempura
Prepare basic recipe, using just 6 red plums and 6 apricots. Mix together 1 1/2 ounces finely chopped hazelnuts, 1 tablespoon light brown sugar, and 3 tablespoons cream cheese. Halve the fruit, remove the pits, and sandwich the halves back together with the hazelnut mixture.

fruit tempura with sesame seed batter
Prepare basic recipe, adding 1 tablespoon white or black sesame seeds to batter with the dry ingredients.

fruit tempura with anise seed batter
Prepare basic recipe. Add 2 teaspoons anise seeds to batter.

variations

blueberry fritters & apricot sauce

see base recipe page 234

berry fritters with golden plum & maple sauce
Prepare basic recipe, replacing apricots in sauce with pitted yellow plums.
Instead of honey, use maple syrup, adding a little extra to taste, if necessary.

minted berry fritters with apricot sauce
Prepare basic recipe, adding 2 teaspoons chopped fresh mint to the
fritter batter.

banana and raspberry fritters with apricot sauce
Prepare basic recipe, replacing blueberries with 1 medium banana, peeled
and chopped.

spiced berry fritters with apricot sauce
Prepare basic recipe, adding 1 teaspoon pumpkin pie spice to fritter batter.

pineapple fritters with apricot sauce
Prepare basic recipe, replacing blueberries and raspberries with 3 fresh or
canned pineapple rings, blotted with paper towels to remove excess juice, and
chopped into small pieces.

variations

chinese toffee pineapple & bananas

see base recipe page 237

chinese toffee pineapple & bananas with fennel seeds
Prepare basic recipe, greasing plate with a mild oil such as sunflower and adding 1 tablespoon fennel seeds rather than sesame seeds to the caramel.

chinese toffee apples
Prepare basic recipe, replacing pineapple and bananas with 3 dessert apples peeled, cored, and cut into 8 wedges each.

nutty chinese toffee pineapple & bananas
Prepare basic recipe, replacing sesame seeds with 3 tablespoons chopped mixed nuts.

gingered chinese toffee pineapple and bananas
Prepare basic recipe, adding 1 teaspoon ground ginger to flour when making the batter. Replace sesame seeds with finely sliced julienne strips of gingerroot.

chinese toffee pears
Prepare basic recipe, replacing pineapple and bananas with 2 ripe but firm pears, peeled, cored, and cut into 6 wedges each, and 1 Asian pear, peeled, cored, and cut into 8 wedges.

variations

Thai coconut balls with watermelon, star fruit & pomegranate seeds

see base recipe page 238

thai coconut balls with lemongrass syrup
Prepare basic recipe. Omit coconut flavoring from syrup. Heat 1 stalk lemongrass, crushed, with sugar and water. Let cool before straining.

thai ginger & lime balls
Prepare basic recipe, replacing coconut milk powder with cow's milk powder and cow's milk in dough balls. Replace coconut flavoring in syrup with half-inch piece gingerroot, shredded, and grated zest and juice of 1 lime.

thai coconut balls with rosewater syrup
Prepare basic recipe, replacing coconut flavoring in syrup with 1/2 teaspoon rosewater and scattering rose petals over the fruit before serving.

thai coconut balls with orange syrup
Prepare basic recipe, replacing coconut flavoring in syrup with finely grated zest and juice of 1 orange.

thai coconut balls with star anise & cinnamon syrup
Prepare basic recipe, adding 2 whole star anise and 1 cinnamon stick, broken into 2 or 3 pieces, to sugar and water when making syrup.

cinnamon beignets with blueberry sauce

see base recipe page 241

spiced beignets with blackberry sauce
Prepare basic recipe, replacing cinnamon with 1 teaspoon pumpkin pie spice.

cinnamon beignets with apricot sauce
Prepare basic recipe, serving beignets with apricot, rather than blackberry, sauce. To make sauce, simmer 6 ounces dried apricots with 2 cups freshly squeezed orange juice in a covered pan for 10 minutes, until apricots are soft. Purée apricots with juice, diluting with extra juice or water if necessary.

ginger beignets with blackberry sauce
Prepare basic recipe, replacing cinnamon with 1 teaspoon ground ginger.

blueberry beignets
Prepare basic recipe, stirring 4 ounces blueberries, dusted lightly with flour, into beignet batter. Serve cooked beignets with Greek yogurt rather than blackberry sauce.

banana beignets with blackberry sauce
Prepare basic recipe, stirring 1 small banana, peeled, chopped, and dusted lightly with flour, into beignet batter.

variations

orange crêpes with pears & grapes

see base recipe page 242

chocolate crêpes with pears & grapes
Prepare basic recipe, replacing 1 tablespoon flour with cocoa powder.

orange crêpes with lemon sauce
Prepare basic recipe for sauce, replacing oranges with 3 large lemons. Cut zest from 1 lemon into fine strips and squeeze juice from all lemons into a pan, adding 4 ounces sugar. Cook gently until sugar dissolves, then stir in butter until melted.

orange crêpes with strawberries & strawberry sauce
Prepare basic recipe, replacing pears and grapes with 9 ounces strawberries, hulled and sliced. Replace orange sauce with strawberry sauce, made by puréeing 9 ounces strawberries with 1 tablespoon lemon juice, 2 tablespoons sugar and 1 tablespoon orange liqueur.

lemon crêpes with blueberries
Prepare basic recipe, replacing orange zest in crêpes with grated zest of 1 large lemon. Replace pears and grapes in sauce with 9 ounces blueberries.

cinnamon orange crêpes
Prepare basic recipe, adding 1 teaspoon ground cinnamon to crêpe batter.

variations

choc 'n' nut crêpes

see base recipe page 245

strawberry & pistachio crêpes
Prepare basic recipe, replacing chocolate sauce with strawberry coulis (page 24) and the pine nuts with chopped pistachios.

double choc 'n' nut crêpes
Prepare basic recipe for crêpes, replacing 1 teaspoon flour with cocoa.

chocolate coconut & mango crêpes
Prepare basic recipe, replacing raspberries with chopped mango and the pine nuts with freshly grated coconut.

choc 'n' pear crepes
Prepare basic recipe for crêpes. Peel, core, and chop 2 pears. Melt 2 ounces sweet butter in a pan. Stir in 2 tablespoons sugar and cook until starting to caramelize. Add pears, toss until coated with juices, and spoon over crêpes. Drizzle with chocolate sauce and sprinkle with pine nuts. Omit raspberries.

chocolate chip waffles

see base recipe page 246

chocolate chip & banana waffles with amaretto chocolate sauce
Prepare the basic waffles, adding 1 mashed ripe banana to the wet
ingredients. Add 1 tablespoon amaretto to the sauce.

chocolate chip & peanut butter waffles with honey peanut butter syrup
Prepare the basic waffles, adding 1/4 cup creamy peanut butter, loosened
with a little heavy cream, to the wet ingredients. For the syrup, over low
heat, mix 1 cup honey and 1/2 cup creamy peanut butter, stirring until
smooth and warm.

chocolate chip & strawberry waffles with strawberry sauce
Prepare the basic waffles, adding 1/4 cup chopped strawberries. For
the sauce, mix 1 tablespoon cornstarch with 3 tablespoons sugar and
1/2 cup orange juice. Over medium heat, add 2 cups chopped strawberries,
2 tablespoons strawberry jam, and 1 tablespoon light corn syrup. Heat gently
until boiling, stirring. Simmer for a minute or two, or until berries have
broken down and sauce is thickened.

made in minutes

If you think you've no time to prepare a proper

dessert, think again. This chapter has lots of

delicious treats that can be prepared in minutes.

Great for quick family meals, and many are

impressive enough to serve at a dinner party too.

toffee, pear & amaretti sundaes

see variations page 273

A quick and easy dessert that's pure indulgence and just what you need to pick you up after a hard day. For an even faster result, use a bought toffee or butterscotch sauce or dulce de leche rather than make your own.

for the toffee sauce
1/2 cup (3 1/2 oz.) whipping cream
3 tbsp. (1 1/2 oz.) unsalted butter
40g (1 1/2 oz.) dark brown sugar
3 tbsp. light corn syrup

for the sundaes
4 scoops chocolate ice cream
4 pear halves, fresh or canned, chopped
6 amaretti, coarsely crushed
4 scoops vanilla ice cream

To make the toffee sauce, place cream, butter, sugar, and corn syrup in a pan. Heat gently until butter, sugar, and syrup melt, stirring occasionally until smooth. Set aside to cool.

To assemble the sundaes, place a scoop of chocolate ice cream in the bottom of 4 sundae glasses. Drizzle with half the cooled toffee sauce. Add half the chopped pears and half the crushed amaretti. Add vanilla ice cream and remaining pears. Drizzle with remaining toffee sauce. Scatter the rest of the amaretti on top and serve.

Serves 4

sticky fruit kebabs with lemon mascarpone

see variations page 274

When the weather is warm, these fresh fruit skewers can be cooked on a barbecue. Be careful, however, not to baste them too liberally with butter and maple syrup, because any that drips into the ashes could cause the coals to flare and scorch the lovely fruit.

for the lemon mascarpone
5 1/2 oz. mascarpone
finely grated zest of 1 lemon
for the kebabs
12 whole strawberries

2 peaches, pitted and cut into thick wedges
2 bananas, peeled and cut into 1 1/2-inch slices
2 figs, each cut into 6 wedges
6 tbsp. (3 oz.) unsalted butter, melted
4 tbsp. maple syrup

To make the lemon mascarpone, stir together mascarpone and half the lemon zest. Spoon into a small bowl and sprinkle remaining zest on top. Cover with plastic wrap and chill until needed.

Preheat the barbecue or a conventional grill to high heat. To make the kebabs, divide strawberries, peach wedges, banana slices, and fig wedges between 8 small skewers. Place skewers side by side on a foil-lined grill rack. Brush fruit with melted butter and half of the maple syrup. Grill for about 5 minutes, turning skewers over several times, and brushing with any juices that are left. Remove from the grill, drizzle with remaining maple syrup, and serve hot with the lemon mascarpone.

Serves 4

nutty chocolate banana sticks

see variations page 275

A party treat for all ages! These can be served on their own or with ice cream.

9 oz. good-quality milk chocolate, chopped
3/4 cup (3 oz.) chopped mixed nuts,
   lightly toasted

2 large bananas
strawberries or Cape gooseberries,
   to serve

Put chopped chocolate in a heatproof bowl and microwave on low power for about 5 minutes or until chocolate has melted. Stir until smooth.

Spread out nuts on a plate.

Peel bananas and cut into 1 1/2-inch lengths. Using a fork, dip each piece of banana into the melted chocolate until coated. Sprinkle with nuts and place on a baking sheet lined with foil or parchment paper. Push a toothpick into each banana piece and leave in a cool place (not the fridge) until set.

Add a strawberry and Cape gooseberry to each toothpick. Serve on their own or with ice cream.

Serves 4

snowy berries with yogurt & toasted oats

see variations page 276

For an even quicker recipe, substitute the toasted oat mixture with bought granola. Break up any large clumps by putting the cereal in a plastic bag and crushing with a rolling pin.

1 tbsp. unsalted butter
1 cup (3 oz.) rolled oats
4 tbsp. (2 oz.) chopped hazelnuts
2 tbsp. light brown sugar
7 oz. natural Greek yogurt

2 tbsp. honey
finely grated zest of 1 small orange
6 oz. fresh raspberries
6 oz. fresh blueberries
confectioners' sugar, to dust

Melt butter in a skillet (preferably nonstick). Add oats and hazelnuts and cook for 1-2 minutes until lightly toasted, stirring frequently. Sprinkle with the brown sugar and cook for another minute, then remove from heat and let cool.

Stir yogurt, honey, and orange zest together. Layer raspberries, blueberries, yogurt, and oat mixture in 4 dessert glasses, finishing with fruit and a light sprinkling of oats.

Chill until ready to serve. Dust with confectioners' sugar just before serving.

Serves 4

maple-glazed pineapple & nectarines with toasted brioche

see variations page 277

You can use fresh or canned pineapple slices for this dessert but, if using canned, look for fruit canned in juice rather than in syrup.

4 tbsp. (2 oz.) butter
6 tbsp. maple syrup
juice of 1 lemon
4 pineapple slices, each cut into 4 pieces

2 large ripe nectarines, pitted and sliced
4-8 slices brioche, depending on size
4 tbsp. lemon curd (page 109)
4 tbsp. dark rum

Heat butter in a large skillet over low heat. When melted, stir in maple syrup and lemon juice. Add pineapple and nectarine slices and cook gently for 5 minutes, spooning cooking juices over the fruit.

Meanwhile, lightly toast brioche slices and spread them with the lemon curd.

Pour rum over fruit and cook for 30 seconds. Place brioche on serving plates and cover with fruit and juices from the pan. Serve immediately.

Serves 4

roasted peaches with ricotta, pistachios & honey

see variations page 278

A simple dessert that's easy to make but stylish enough to serve for a special lunch or dinner party. Soft amaretti would make a good accompaniment.

4 ripe peaches, halved and pitted
4 tbsp. (2 oz.) unsalted butter, melted
2 tbsp. brown sugar
2 tbsp. honey

2 tsp. lemon juice
5 1/2 oz. ricotta cheese
2 tbsp. coarsely chopped pistachios

Preheat the oven to 425°F. Place peach halves, cut sides up, side by side in a shallow roasting pan. Drizzle or brush with melted butter. Sprinkle with sugar and roast for 10 minutes.

Stir honey and lemon juice together. As soon as peaches come out of the oven, transfer them to serving plates, top each half with a spoonful of ricotta, and sprinkle with pistachios. Serve drizzled with the lemon honey.

Serves 4

peach & popcorn glories

see variations page 279

You'll need to make up the gelatin a few hours ahead so it can set, but once it is firm these glamorous sundaes can be assembled in seconds. You can buy the strawberry dessert sauce, but if you have time you can make your own using the recipe on page 24.

1/2 package orange gelatin
4 peach halves, fresh or canned
1 1/2 cups (2 oz.) caramel popcorn

strawberry dessert sauce
8 scoops strawberry ice cream
chocolate shapes, to decorate

Make gelatin according to package instructions and pour it into a shallow container lined with plastic wrap. Chill to set, then turn out, peel off plastic wrap, and chop gelatin into small cubes.

Chop peaches into small dice. Spoon a little orange gelatin and some of the popcorn into 4 sundae glasses. Add some of the peaches, a little strawberry sauce, and a scoop of strawberry ice cream. Add more orange gelatin, peach, and popcorn, and finish with scoops of ice cream and strawberry sauce.

Serve at once decorated with chocolate shapes.

Serves 6

Eton mess

see variations page 280

This traditional English dessert is said to have originated during the 1930s on the playing fields of Eton College, where it was served at the picnic held at the end of May to celebrate the annual prize giving. To begin with, it was just cream and fruit. Some say the "mess" was created when a Labrador retriever sat on the picnic basket. The meringues were a later addition.

1 lb. fresh strawberries, plus extra for
   decoration
3 tbsp. orange juice

4 meringue baskets or 8 small meringue shells
scant 1 cup (7 fl. oz.) heavy cream
7 oz. Greek yogurt

Hull strawberries. Reserve half of them and purée the rest with orange juice in a food processor or blender.

Chop meringues into small pieces.

Whip cream until it holds its shape, then stir in the yogurt. Slice or chop reserved strawberries and fold them into cream mixture along with meringue pieces. Divide between 4 serving glasses, layering mixture with strawberry purée. Serve decorated with extra strawberries.

Serves 4

baked plums & apples with caramelized cinnamon topping

see variations page 281

As the dish needs to go into the oven as well as under the broiler, choose one that you're sure is heatproof and not your best china!

12 oz. plums, halved or quartered and pitted
2 apples, peeled, cored, and sliced or chopped
4 tbsp. (2 oz.) unsalted butter, cut up
5 tbsp. light brown sugar
1/2 cup heavy cream

1 (6-oz.) container whole milk apricot or lemon yogurt
2 tbsp. fresh or dried bread crumbs
1 tsp. ground cinnamon

Preheat oven to 350°F. Spread out plums and apple slices in a shallow heatproof dish or pie pan and dot with butter. Sprinkle with 2 tablespoons brown sugar and bake for 15–20 minutes or until the fruit has softened a little but still holds its shape.

Whip cream until thickened, stir in yogurt, and spoon over the fruit, spreading it in an even layer. Mix together the remaining brown sugar, bread crumbs, and cinnamon, and sprinkle over the top. Slide dish under the broiler for 4–5 minutes or until the sugar caramelizes. Serve warm or cold.

Serves 4

variations

toffee, pear & amaretti sundaes

see base recipe page 257

toffee, apricot & ginger sundaes
Prepare basic recipe, replacing amaretti with gingersnaps and the pears
with apricots.

toffee, pear & coffee sundaes
Prepare basic recipe, replacing chocolate ice cream with coffee ice cream and
the amaretti with chopped nuts.

chocolate, pear & amaretti sundaes
Prepare basic recipe, replacing toffee sauce with chocolate sauce (page 24).

red berries & amaretti sundaes
Prepare basic recipe, replacing pears with 8 ounces fresh raspberries. Replace
toffee sauce with strawberry sauce made by puréeing 8 ounces fresh strawberries
with 1/2 cup orange juice (or use a store-bought sauce). Replace chocolate ice
cream with strawberry ice cream.

variations

sticky fruit kebabs with lemon mascarpone

see base recipe page 258

sticky fruit & marshmallow kebabs
Prepare basic recipe, adding marshmallows to skewers, alternating with
fruit pieces.

sticky fruit kebabs with boozy mascarpone
Prepare basic recipe, adding a splash of limoncello to lemon mascarpone.

honeyed fruit kebabs with lemon mascarpone
Prepare basic recipe, replacing maple syrup with honey.

sticky fruit kebabs with brandy cream
Prepare basic recipe, replacing lemon mascarpone with brandy cream. Whip
1/2 cup heavy cream with 2 tablespoons brandy and 1 tablespoon sugar.

variations

nutty chocolate banana sticks

see base recipe page 260

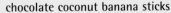

chocolate coconut banana sticks
Prepare basic recipe, replacing nuts with lightly toasted flaked coconut.

nutty chocolate strawberry sticks
Prepare basic recipe, replacing bananas with 12 large strawberries and the mixed nuts with finely chopped hazelnuts.

nutty dark chocolate banana sticks
Prepare basic recipe, replacing milk chocolate with dark chocolate.

sesame chocolate banana sticks
Prepare basic recipe, replacing chopped nuts with sesame seeds.

variations

snowy berries with yogurt & toasted oats

see base recipe page 262

snowy berries with whiskey cream & oats
Prepare basic recipe, replacing yogurt with 1 scant cup heavy cream whipped until thick with 2 tablespoons whiskey and 1 tablespoon confectioners' sugar.

snowy berries with yogurt & sunflower seeds
Prepare basic recipe, replacing oats with sunflower seeds.

snowy midnight berries with yogurt & toasted oats
Prepare basic recipe, replacing raspberries with blackberries.

snowy berries with ricotta & toasted oats
Prepare basic recipe, replacing yogurt with ricotta cheese.

variations

maple-glazed pineapple & nectarines with toasted brioche

see base recipe page 265

maple-glazed pineapple & nectarines with almonds & raisins
Prepare basic recipe, adding 2 tablespoons chopped almonds and
2 tablespoons raisins to pan with the fruit.

maple-glazed pineapple & nectarines with chocolate brioche
Prepare basic recipe, spreading brioche with chocolate hazelnut spread
rather than lemon curd.

honey-glazed pineapple & nectarines with toasted brioche
Prepare basic recipe, replacing maple syrup with 5 tablespoons honey.

maple-glazed oranges & cherries with toasted brioche
Prepare basic recipe, replacing pineapple with 2 large oranges, peeled and
sliced, and the nectarines with 9 ounces pitted cherries.

variations

roasted peaches with ricotta, pistachios & honey

see base recipe page 266

roasted apricots with ricotta, pistachios & honey
Prepare basic recipe, replacing peaches with 8 apricots.

roasted peaches with mascarpone, pistachios & honey
Prepare basic recipe, replacing ricotta with mascarpone.

roasted plums with ricotta, pistachios & honey
Prepare basic recipe, replacing peaches with 8 large firm plums.

roasted peaches with ricotta, walnuts & maple syrup
Prepare basic recipe, replacing pistachios with walnuts and the honey with maple syrup.

peach & popcorn glories

see base recipe page 269

raspberry & popcorn glories
Prepare basic recipe, using raspberry gelatin instead of orange and 6 ounces fresh raspberries instead of peaches.

peach, chocolate & popcorn glories
Prepare basic recipe, using chocolate ice cream instead of strawberry, and chocolate sauce (page 24) instead of strawberry sauce.

peach, butterscotch & popcorn glories
Prepare basic recipe, replacing caramel popcorn with plain sweet popcorn, orange gelatin with lemon, and strawberry ice cream with vanilla. Replace strawberry dessert sauce with butterscotch sauce.

peach & honeycomb glories
Prepare basic recipe, replacing half the popcorn with 1 bar chocolate-covered honeycomb (such as Toblerone Honey Crisp), coarsely chopped.

variations

Eton mess

see base recipe page 270

frozen Eton mess gâteau
Prepare basic recipe, spooning mixture into a loaf pan or round cake pan and pressing down in an even layer. Freeze for several hours or overnight until solid. Transfer to the fridge 30–45 minutes before serving to give the dessert time to soften but not defrost.

peach & blueberry mess
Prepare basic recipe, replacing strawberries with blueberries.

peach, red berry & chocolate mess
Prepare basic recipe, replacing half the strawberries with raspberries and drizzling with chocolate sauce just before serving.

nutty Eton mess
Prepare basic recipe, folding 3 tablespoons chopped toasted almonds into whipped cream with strawberries and meringues.

variations

baked plums & apples with caramelized cinnamon topping

see base recipe page 272

baked pears & peaches with cinnamon topping
Prepare basic recipe, using 2 pears instead of apples and 12 ounces peaches instead of plums.

baked plums & apples with mascarpone topping
Prepare basic recipe, replacing heavy cream with 7 ounces mascarpone used straight from the container.

baked plums & apples with nutty ginger topping
Prepare basic recipe, replacing bread crumbs with chopped mixed nuts and the cinnamon with ground ginger.

baked plums & apricots with cinnamon topping
Prepare basic recipe, replacing apples with 8 apricots, halved and pitted.

index

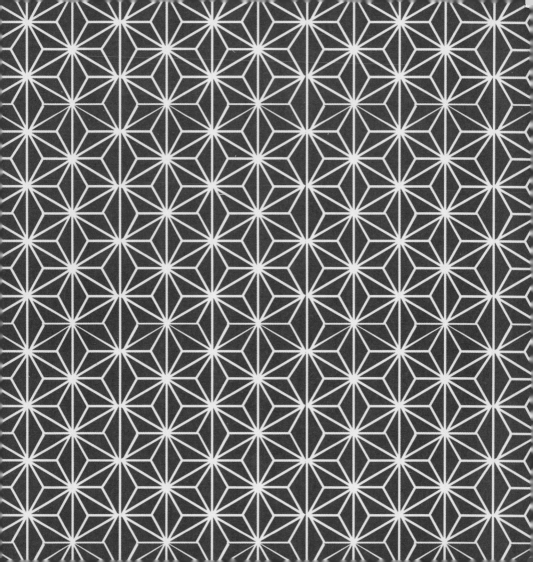

>>>>>>>>>> PLAYS OF IMPASSE <<<<<<<<<<